LifeWriting

LifeWriting

Drawing from
Personal Experience
to
Create Features
You Can Publish

Fred D. White, Ph.D.

Sanger, California

Printed in the United States of America
Published by Quill Driver Books/Word Dancer Press, Inc.
1831 Industrial Way #101
Sanger, California 93657
559-876-2170 • 1-800-497-4909 • FAX 559-876-2180
QuillDriverBooks.com
Info@QuillDriverBooks.com

Quill Driver Books' titles may be purchased in quantity at special discounts for educational, fund-raising, business, or promotional use. Please contact Special Markets, Quill Driver Books/Word Dancer Press, Inc. at the above address or at **1-800-497-4909**.

Quill Driver Books/Word Dancer Press, Inc. project cadre:
Susan Klassen, John David Marion, Cheree McCloud, Stephen Blake Mettee,
Brigitte Phillips, Linda Kay Weber

First Printing

To order another copy of this book, please call
1-800-497-4909

Library of Congress Cataloging-in-Publication Data

White, Fred D., 1943-
Lifewriting : drawing from personal experience to create features you can publish / by Fred
D. White.
p. cm.
Includes index.
ISBN 1-884956-33-5
1. Feature writing. 2. Autobiography--Authorship. I. Title.

PN4784.F37W48 22004
808'.02--dc22
2004003527

For Therese

Writing is making sense of life

—Nadine Gordimer

Contents

Part Three: Lifewriting Projects

Part Four: Developing Your Style

Part Five: Shepherding Your Lifewriting Essays into Print or Cyberspace

Introduction

This is a book on how to succeed at lifewriting—my term of choice for people-centered nonfiction writing; not just autobiographical or biographical portraits or memoirs, but personal-experience narratives, exposés, and lively features about crafts, hobbies, travel, pilgrimages, recreational activities, and human relations. Lifewriting can be serious or humorous or both. It can include any kind of subject-matter because people are always at the heart of any lifewriting endeavor, from theoretical physics to circus performing to ghost hunting in medieval Scottish castles. It can be written for any audience, from preschool children to retirees.

Regardless of your background, your level of education; regardless of your life experiences, you can master the skills of lifewriting and publish your work. There is only one prerequisite and you already know what it is: a willingness to work hard at your writing. This willingness to commit yourself to a serious writing work ethic covers the following ground:

- Forming a daily habit of writing
- Keeping a writer's daybook
- Understanding the activities of composing: planning, researching, drafting, revising, and copyediting
- Learning how to market your work

This book will guide you carefully through each of these stages.

The Need for Good Writing

People have an insatiable need to understand their world, their fellow human beings, and themselves, and for that reason they have an equally insatiable desire to read articles and books that will provide that understanding. Good writing is forever in high demand—and with good reason: It isn't easy to write well. As with any activity, to become a good writer you have to practice continually.

I teach college-level writing for a living, and I have some insight into what it takes to acquire competence as a writer. For one thing, a single course in composition is not enough. To be a good writer, students must write as often as possible in other contexts, not just other courses, but in daily life. They must learn to think and observe like writers—that is, they must no longer be content with superficial definitions or explanations or arguments. When observing, they must look for nuances, for those intricacies and subtleties of life so easily overlooked. They must learn to compare and contrast and understand cause and effect relationships.

There is another aspect of writing that often gets overlooked in college writing courses, and which I take pains to include in this book: the soul-nurturing, pleasurable, intellectually, emotionally invigorating—and *creative* side. *Creative* is one of those lovely words that speaks to the pleasures of imagination, to the freedom of individual expression and insight. I have always felt that learning of any kind, at any level from nursery school to graduate school, is likelier to succeed when it is pleasurable, and essay writing is no exception. It's a misconception, and a dangerous one, that reason and emotion are opposing, even warring, factions of the human psyche. A new concept can stir up emotions. A powerful emotion can help solve a problem. Our life experiences are comprised of thinking and feeling intertwined.

How do writers get their essays written? Quite often, they get so worked up over an idea, the essay practically writes itself. For example, a woman suffers a traumatic experience that profoundly changes her life (let's say this person was robbed at gunpoint)—and she can barely contain her rage, her feeling of being violated, her sense that she had come within a hair's breath of being murdered or severely incapacitated. After the mind-numbing shock wears off, a powerful impulse arises: She must share this experience with others—not just by talking about it, but by writing about it. Why is that? Perhaps partly because of altruistic reasons. Most of us do rush to the aid of people in need, and sharing experiences is a way of aiding others. But an even stronger reason is the need to probe deeply into an experience in order make meaning out of it—and writing is an effective way to do this.

The biggest challenge is not what to write about, but how to draw material out of your past and present experiences, as well as the past and present experiences of others, and shape this material into features that will engage a large public (which is where the word "publish" comes from).

How To Use This Book

LifeWriting is designed for self-instruction. While it is slanted for the novice, there is nothing elementary or school-bookish about the contents, or about the activities and exercises you will be asked to perform. Your imagination and your creativity will be challenged every step of the way.

Which leads me to four preliminary bits of advice.

First, decide on where you want your writing space to be. It should be comfortable, with adequate lighting, ventilation, and room for books and a desk or table with room enough to spread out materials.

Second, don't skip or slight any of the activities. Read the chapters more-or-less in sequence, especially the first ten chapters, and complete the activities, including the exercises at the end of most chapters.

Third, plan to review the material—and do the activities—more than once. You'll absorb more; your writing will change, evolve, and redefine itself, and that's good. Learning to write can be described as a process of discovering one's inner resources—and sometimes that discovery consists of many smaller discoveries and re-discoveries.

Fourth, and most important of all, believe in yourself as a writer. Once you start putting pen to paper—or fingers to keyboard—on a regular basis, you are a writer. The fact that you work at your craft every day—not whether you publish—is the mark of a writer. That alone will not guarantee your getting published, but you cannot get published any other way. I've encountered many would-be writers with a rich hoard of essay ideas, a lifetime of fascinating experiences under their belts, and a flair for language to boot—would-be writers who dream of "writing a heck of a story one of these days"—but they are not yet writers because they lack the drive to sit down, day after day after day, even when their friends are out having fun, getting those ideas and experiences down on paper. Are *you* one of those non-writers who talk about how successful a writer you could be if you only had the time? If so, I hope you saved the receipt for this book so you can return it for a refund.

Unless you make up your mind that you're going to write on a regular basis, nothing you will read in the following pages will be of use to you.

What? You're going to write every day, come hell or high water? Then I congratulate you on your resolve. Your journey toward becoming a writer is well underway.

Now roll up your sleeves, do some stretching exercises, put the aspirin where it's handy, and get ready to work.

Part One

Building the Foundation

1

Getting Started on Your Lifewriting Adventure

In this Chapter
~ Anatomy of lifewriting
~ A brief history of lifewriting
~ Cultivating good writing habits
~ Subjects for lifewriting
~ Celebrating yourself
~ The art of brainstorming
~ The art of titles

You are about to embark on an intellectually stimulating adventure—that of learning the art of writing emotionally-charged essays based on your experiences or the experiences of others. In this kind of essay writing—what I refer to as *lifewriting*, you draw from your unique set of experiences, your own special way of perceiving and interacting with the world. You allow yourself the freedom to express your likes and dislikes, your tastes and values. Unlike more reportorial forms of nonfiction in which such freedom of personal expressiveness is discouraged, lifewriting is shaped by it.

Anatomy of Lifewriting

Lifewriting sometimes goes by other names, such as "biography," "memoir," "personal essay," "feature," or "creative nonfiction"—but these terms do not convey the purpose of such writing, which is to entertain and edify readers with stories about your experiences, or the experiences of others as informed through your own perspective.

So, let's settle on a clear-cut definition of lifewriting: It is a lively, dramatic, sometimes witty, relatively short (generally between 500 and 4,000 words—the smaller pieces being more suitable for newspapers) or book-length prose on a person or person-centered topic, targeted for a wide readership.

The great thing about lifewriting is that you do not have to worry about whether you have anything worth writing about. Anyone who has "survived childhood," as Flannery O'Connor once said, has enough material for a lifetime of writing. It's true! and you'll have a chance to prove it to yourself shortly.

To succeed at lifewriting you do have to learn a few things about *technique*—how to convey your experiences on the page in a way that your audience will take pleasure in reading and from which they will learn something. Lifewriting technique is what you are going to learn from this book.

A Brief History of Lifewriting

Lifewriting can be traced back to ancient Rome. Seneca (A.D. 3–65), the Stoic philosopher and tutor of Nero, wrote letters that were very much like essays in the modern sense. Here is an excerpt from his ruminations about "Asthma":

> Even as I fought for breath...I never ceased to find comfort in cheerful and courageous reflections. "What's this?" I said. "So death is having all these tries at me, is he? Let him, then! I had a try at him a long while ago myself."
>
> Translated by Robin Campbell; from *The Art of the Personal Essay*, ed. Philip Lopate. Anchor Books/Doubleday, 1994.

There were also writers in China a thousand years ago who produced lifewriting. The Sung Dynasty poet, Ou-Yang Hsiu (1007–1072), for example, participated in a tradition of writing personal impressions of landscapes.

However, it is the French writer Michel de Montaigne (1533–1592), a contemporary of Shakespeare, who is considered to be the father of the essay. He coined the word, from the French *essayer*, meaning to try, to attempt, to take a stab at something, to come to terms with an idea or situation from a strictly personal perspective. Montaigne liked writing on a vast range of topics: on the education of children, on cannibalism, on growing old, on reading books—often shamelessly sharing his own biases and shortcomings with the reader.

But lifewriting didn't fully flourish until modern times. E. B. White, famous for his children's book *Charlotte's Web*, wrote gentle satires about modern foibles and the passing of traditional ways of life, as well as lyrical reflections on relationships between parents and children. James Thurber, one of the greatest humorists of the twentieth century, poked fun at commonplace customs like dating. George Orwell, best known for *Nineteen Eighty-Four*, his nightmare vision of life in a future totalitarian society, captured the ugliness of imperialism and tyranny in many of his journalistic pieces. M. F. K. Fisher wrote rhapsodically about the pleasures of eating. Once we start discussing the techniques of lifewriting, we will examine passages written by these masters.

Cultivating Good Writing Habits

Before we get into technique, though, let's consider some basic habits of writing you need to cultivate.

1. Take time to write every day.

The most important part of learning to write is to *write*—regularly, habitually. So, if you're not sure you can spend at least a small amount of time (thirty minutes to an hour) putting words on paper each day, you'd better return this book to the library or bookstore now. The easiest excuse a would-be writer can make is, "Gosh, I'm so busy that I don't have *time* to write." If you truly want to become a writer, then you must promise yourself never to make that excuse.

2. Write with worthy writer-based and reader-based motives in mind.

People sometimes want to write for the wrong reasons: to impress people, to get rich and famous, to get even. These *writer*-based motives should be secondary at best. Better (i.e., more serviceable) writer-based motives might include a desire to draw attention to an unsung hero in your family, or to publicize some of your proud achievements as a carpenter or lawyer or tennis player or a nurturing and mentoring parent.

But there are also *reader*-based motives to consider. By keeping readers' interests in mind (for example, emphasizing facets of your topic that would have widespread use or appeal), you will have a better chance of getting your writing published.

3. Give yourself plenty of time to revise your work.

Revising is fundamental to the composing process, and it is much more than "correcting." As the word itself implies, it also means re-seeing your work from a fresh and objective perspective. You will learn about revising methods in Chapter 10.

4. Think and observe like a writer.

It is often said that for a writer, everything is potential material. Without getting obsessive about it, thinking about the possibilities of transforming your experiences into essays will sharpen your powers of observation. To capitalize on writing-project opportunities, writers keep notebooks. This is one of the most important activities for a writer, as I will explain in the next chapter.

5. Try to unlearn wrong-headed ideas about writing.

If your earliest encounters with writing have been anything like mine, the very word "writing" (or "essay," or "theme,") may send chills up your spine. Perhaps you were suddenly reminded of that high school English teacher who slashed your essays to pieces with gashes of red ink and deducted points for violating so-called rules of essay writing ("You can't use the word 'I'; "Every paragraph must begin with a topic sentence"; "Do not use contractions"; "An essay should be five paragraphs long"; blah blah blah). Such experiences have taught legions of young people only one thing about writing: how to avoid it at all costs.

Outmoded Notions about Writing

• *You can't use the word "I."* This probably came about because beginning writers sometimes refer to themselves unnecessarily: "In my opinion I think that grades should be abolished." Better to say, "Grades should be abolished,"since it is obvious the writer is thinking that, and that she is expressing her opinion. This "rule" has been seriously misinterpreted as "You're not supposed to refer to yourself in an essay"—and that often defeats the purpose of essay writing. (See the sidebar on page 11, "Thoreau on Writing in the First Person.")

• *An essay must be five paragraphs long.* Nonsense, as picking up virtually any magazine will prove. "The five-paragraph theme" as it notoriously became known, is a useful exercise, however—training wheels, so to speak, for students who have never written an essay before. One introduces the topic in the first paragraph, discusses three aspects concerning the topic in the next three paragraphs, and then wraps things up with a concluding paragraph. Experienced writers do not count paragraphs. If it turns out that their essays are five paragraphs long, so be it. Joan Didion's essay, "Marrying Absurd," examined in depth in Chapter 17, is five paragraphs long—but ironically (in this masterful essay filled with ironies), her paragraph structure is as unconventional as can be.

• *Never use slang ("cool"), contractions ("don't"), begin a sentence with a conjunction ("and" or "because") or end them with a preposition ("into").* This rule probably came about because teachers wanted students to practice correct grammar and usage at all times. But personal essays are supposed to be informal and colloquial, dude. Hey, it's cool to use these things if writing in an informal manner is what you're into.

Lifewriting is a celebration of yourself and others, a declaration of your creative independence. You write what you want to write and how you want to write it—mindful of your readers' interests and expectations, of course. You want to do all you can to help readers enjoy the morsels of wit and wisdom that you're feeding them.

Artistic freedom carries artistic responsibility. Readers appreciate innovation and eccentricity, but be sure you give them enough cues to follow along. Once they start scratching their heads and muttering "huh?", you'll lose them. Remember Humpty Dumpty in *Through the Looking Glass*? He arrogantly assumed he could make words mean whatever he wanted to and, thus nobody had a clue what he was trying to say!

Subjects for Lifewriting

Now let's talk about subject matter. Lifewriting is fun and meaningful because you're writing about yourself and others in the fullest sense of these words: your loves and hates (or those of someone close to you), people's faults and eccentricities (including your own), effective or ineffective ways of interacting with people; how people feel about their jobs; courtship customs in different cultures; why you enjoy eating crab legs or licorice or serving cherries jubilee to guests or wearing crazy ties or oversized, exotic earrings; what it was like taking a pilgrimage to the wild west coast of Ireland, and how it changed your life; why foreign language study is so important—and what you can do, as a parent or teacher, to capitalize on young children's amazing ability to learn a second language; why listening to Ella Fitzgerald singing Cole Porter casts a romantic spell over you; or what on earth ever motivated you to keep a boa constrictor for a pet.

In other words, when you write about your experiences, you don't hold back on your strong feelings and attitudes. Share those feelings that likely spurred you into writing in the first place. Readers appreciate candor. Besides, reading enjoyment is likelier to occur when it stirs the reader's heart along his brain.

You also want to get inside the heads of people you're writing about, not just be content with describing them at a distance. Let's say that you want to write a profile of an emergency-room nurse—Mary Jones, whose rapid decision-making and familiarity with lifesaving equipment helped to

Thoreau on Writing in the First Person

Henry David Thoreau (1817–1862), one of the most famous American essayists, audaciously proclaimed in the opening chapter of his masterpiece, *Walden*:

> In most books, the I, or first person, is omitted; in this it will be retained.... We commonly do not remember that it is, after all, always the first person that is speaking.
> I should not talk so much about myself if there were any body else whom I knew as well.

Ol' Henry certainly wasn't about to follow any schoolmarmish rules! It wasn't mere coincidence that he began his two-year stay at Walden Pond on July 4, 1845.

save many lives over the years. Fascinating as it is to see her in action, readers also want to get inside her skin, to know what it feels like to be faced with an E.R. crisis, such as what she must do to help save the life of a teenager hemorrhaging from multiple stab wounds. It may not be enough to interview Nurse Jones; you may need to shadow her in the E.R. for a couple of days, so you can begin to see and comprehend her milieu through her eyes.

Celebrating Yourself

Celebrating yourself may sound at first like the worst kind of self-centeredness—but it really is not. To affirm joyously who you are is a way of inspiring others to embark on the path toward self-fulfillment. Walt Whitman expresses this idea in the opening of "Song of Myself":

> I celebrate myself, and sing myself
> And what I assume you shall assume,
> For every atom belonging to me as good belongs to you.

Far from being egotistical, when you celebrate yourself, you are presenting yourself as a real person, shortcomings and all. Your maladies, handicaps, biases, and tastes all add color to your personality! Besides, readers like and demand candor. The following are some examples of lifewriting that "celebrate" the authentic self in this manner:

- The infirmities and indignities of old age: Montaigne, "Of Age" in *Selected Essays of Michel de Montaigne*
- What it's like to be a counselor to college-prep students: Caitlin Flanagan, "Confessions of a Prep School College Counselor," from *The Best American Magazine Writing*, 2002
- What it's like being an opium addict: Thomas de Quincy, *Confessions of an English Opium Eater*
- Coping with life after a severe brain injury: Floyd Skloot, "Gray Area: Thinking with a Damaged Brain" from *Best American Essays*, 2000
- Feeling envious of others: Joseph Epstein, "A Few Kind Words for Envy," from *Best American Essays*, 1990
- Traveling around the world in search of miracles: Toni Mirosevich, "Lambs of God and the New Math," from *The Best American Travel Writing*, 2002

And, speaking of candor, the hallmark of memorable personal lifewriting is that the authors open themselves up to us for all to see; they are unflinchingly candid about their feelings and attitudes, their strengths and weaknesses. They do not try to make themselves "look good" before the camera, so to speak. They let it all hang out. As the essayist Scott Russell Sanders once put it, "Unlike novelists and playwrights, who lurk behind the scenes...the essayist has nowhere to hide."

Such candor is not as easy to maintain as it might seem. You will have to constantly remind yourself to be forthright, not to hold anything back that would help your readers understand the reality of a circumstance. All of us role play to some extent: We edit our remarks, we put our best face forward. We dread the thought of anyone thinking or speaking disparagingly of us. We're not being phonies when we do this, we just want to make good impressions on others. In the business world, this may well be a necessity, akin to dressing up or wearing makeup. In art, however, it presents a problem. Audiences are keen to pick up what doesn't ring true.

The Art of Brainstorming

With lifewriting, you can write about virtually anything at all. What makes it *lifewriting* is its being rooted in personal experience—your own or someone else's. This human dimension is necessary for commanding a large audience. People in general tend to learn much more about a subject when it has a human-interest slant. Molecular genetics might not be everyone's cup of tea, but James Watson captivated millions of readers when, in *The Double Helix* (1968), he told the story of how he and Francis Crick came to discover the structure of the DNA molecule.

The most common bit of advice beginning writers get is "Write about what you know." This certainly makes good sense, but I would tack on an equally important corollary: Write about what obsesses or excites you— not just interests you, but that which gets you fired up or keeps you awake at night. Watson and Crick had been obsessed for years in their search for the molecular engine responsible for genetic traits and genetic transference— what they considered to be "the secret of life." Their scientific papers revealed nothing of their obsession or even their quest—one doesn't include such things in scientific papers, of course. It's a lot easier to embed the scientific work in the human story than the other way around.

Of course, you don't have to tell a story like Watson's quest for the secret of life to be a successful lifewriter. Most of the experiences we remember are important (that's why we remember them) and can have far-reaching effects. A vast readership exists out there for any life experiences told well. For instance, consider the following as subjects that might elicit a strong reader response:

- Enduring the anguish of mastectomy and learning to live— and prevail in unexpected ways despite the disfigurement and initial shame

- Struggling to save a marriage on the brink of dissolution
- Overcoming obsessive compulsive behavior
- Developing programs that help street people regain control of their lives

We not only learn a lot from reading such experiences, but our own lives become richer in the process.

One good way to decide what to write about is to put together a list of topics over the next few weeks. Don't try assembling such a list all at one time—be patient, and numerous ideas will strike over the course of several days.

Before you get to work on your idea list, though, take a look at what other writers have focused on, just to get a sense of possibilities. The American environmentalist John Muir (1838–1914) wrote about the pleasure he experienced observing birds in Yosemite Valley and while hiking over Alaskan glaciers. In "Notes of a Native Son," the African-American author James Baldwin (1924–1987) captured the rage he felt against white people after being told—one time too many, "We don't serve Negroes here." The naturalist Annie Dillard (b. 1945) captured the surreal and terrifying experience of witnessing a total eclipse of the sun. Robert Louis Stevenson (1850–1894), immortalized by his story, *The Strange Case of Dr. Jekyll and Mr. Hyde*, once wrote an essay in defense of idleness. The Japanese writer Junichiro Tanizaki (1886–1965) wrote a fascinating essay about shadows. The American Pulitzer-prize winning poet Mary Oliver (b. 1935) wrote an essay about dust. One of the best known essays by English writer Virginia Woolf (1882–1941) focuses on the death of a moth, and how it caused her to think deeply about the boundary between life and death, about the fate of circumstance, about the inescapable fact of mortality.

Enough about other writers' ideas. Time now to jot down things that you would enjoy writing about. The key word here is *enjoy*. Without enthusiasm behind your lifewriting, your prose will be as interesting as a pot of overcooked noodles.

Begin by drawing up categories for your essays and jotting down topics and possible approaches to the topic inside each category. Take a sheet of paper and fold it in thirds lengthwise. On the left side, jot down categories. In the center, list topics, and on the right, possible focuses. Remember to put your own personal spin, your own peculiar angle of vision, on the topic. Here are some examples:

Category	Topic	Possible Focus
At Home	Household chores	Untold delights of rearranging furniture
	Child rearing	What it's like to bond with an adopted child
	Garage storage	How I tripled the storage space in my garage
At Leisure	Unusual hobbies	Why I collect obsolete computers
At Work	Coworkers	Impossible to get along with my boss
		Flirting at work
Cravings	Junk Food	Why junk food is important to my life
		First time I went to McDonald's
Family History	A long lost ancestor	Rediscovering my great-great-great Uncle Thomas: Welsh farmer….and composer
Dreams unrealized	Childhood ambition	I wanted to be a doctor when I grew up; so why didn't I?
Moments in history	Visiting Pompeii	The day before Vesuvius blew: daily life in the doomed city
Frightful moments	Being trapped	How I endured being trapped in a hotel elevator for three hours
Travel	Back road vacations	Rediscovering life's simple pleasures in rural Ohio

In the chapters that follow, you will learn how to transform ideas like these into salable features. For now, though, start jotting down as many ideas as you can, to remind yourself of the many possibilities for lifewriting.

You will quickly discover that the mere act of writing things down sharpens your memories and even helps retrieve them. Writing can also improve your ability to produce detailed information you may have forgotten.

The Art of Titles

I urge you to think carefully about the titles you give to your lifewriting features—for two reasons: The title will be the first thing your readers (and your editor!) will notice. You want to capture their attention and curiosity. And, a good title will help you stay in focus as you develop the piece.

A good title does not necessarily mean a fancy or even a clever one. Whatever rouses curiosity will do the trick. Joan Didion's essay about her migraine headaches is titled simply, "In Bed." Very simple, yet readers can't help but wonder what bed-related experience she is referring to. Marcia Aldrich used a single word for the title of her piece, collected in *The Best American Essays*, 1993: "Hair." Like "In Bed," "Hair" is a curiosity-stimulator: Is she referring to the way women (or men) wear their hair in different cultures? The sexual appeal of hair? Hair loss?

Aldrich's essay is about her mother's attitude toward her daughters' hair as they were growing up—as well as toward her own hair. It begins as follows:

> I've been around and seen the Taj Majal and the Grand Canyon and Marilyn Monroe's footprints outside Grauman's Chinese Theater, but I've never seen my mother wash her own hair.

Just as the title goads us into reading the opening sentence, the opening sentence goads us into reading the rest of the essay. We'll look more closely at the art of effective openings in Chapter 7.

EXERCISES

1. Here's a quick way to start accumulating lifewriting ideas. Write down any age from the time when your earliest memories begin to the present. Underneath that age, record, in as much detail as you can, one or more experiences you recall from that year. Do the same with each succeeding age.

2. Take your morning newspaper and write down one or two essay ideas for two or more of the stories and features you find some personal

involvement with or reaction to in each section. When you finish, you should have dozens of lifewriting ideas that will keep you busy for the next several months!

3. Imagine that a friend or relative has asked you why you want to be a writer. Respond in detail to that question in a letter.

4. Write another letter to a close friend in which you relate both the happiest and the saddest moments in your life.

5. Recreate two or three moments when someone embarrassed you, or when you embarrassed yourself. What did it feel like? How did it come about? What short-term consequences did it have? What long-term consequences did it have, and how did these consequences affect your life.

2

Using a Daybook to Hoard Your Treasure Trove of Memories and Reflections

In this Chapter
~ What is a daybook?
~ How to keep a daybook: three easy steps
~ Using your daybook to maximum advantage
~ Acquiring the daybook habit
~ Daybook activities
~ Using your daybook to create people profiles
~ Additional fun things to do with your daybook

With any luck, the first chapter has gotten you thinking in a new, writerly way about your life. Perhaps you realize more than ever before that many aspects of your life—even the "minor" experiences—are worth exploring for the sake of turning them into salable features.

It is time now to introduce you to the most basic of the lifewriter's tools: the daybook.

What Is a Daybook?

Call it a journal, a writer's notebook, a verbal sketch pad or even a quarry because it is where you go to extract the raw ore of ideas in order to turn them into publishable essays. I prefer the word "daybook" because it reminds me that writing should be a daily pursuit, like any professional work, and that the spontaneous, rough, or private writing you place in it comprises a book—in its own right. Because writers work with words—the same stuff that thoughts are made of—they must practice their thinking skills on a regular basis; and what better way to maintain such daily writing than in a daybook (as opposed to trusting them to memory, or to scribbling things down on loose scraps of paper which are easily misplaced or lost).

Thinking like a writer is several notches above ordinary thinking in the sense that such thinking requires keen, detailed observations and well-thought-out ideas. That's why a daybook is so important: It's where you record and preserve and mine those ideas.

Daybooks come in all shapes and sizes. You can opt for a pocket-sized one such as reporters and detectives carry, or a larger daybook that students commonly use for taking notes in class. Smaller daybooks are easier to carry in a pocket or purse; the larger ones, while more capacious, need to be carried under your arm or in a backpack or briefcase.

I use both kinds myself—which can be tricky, because that means I don't have all my daybook entries in one place. But ideas often occur to me when I'm in places where a large notebook would be awkward to carry (if not downright rude), such as at a party. I wouldn't seem very sociable if I started writing away in a large notebook while everyone else was conversing over the artichoke dip; on the other hand, a surreptitious scribble in my pocket-sized notebook probably doesn't raise an eyebrow.

"Comp Books," those 8" x 10" lined notebooks with stiff marble-pattern covers and sewn bindings that cost about $2.00, are ideal. One comp book should last you two or three months, even if you write copiously in it. They're easy to carry, and they're durable.

Some writers enjoy those fancy fabric-covered or laminated art-print notebooks, the kinds you see in bookstores. I myself don't care for them—they're too nice!—making me reluctant to write spontaneously in them, as if my jottings would have to be worthy of those elegant works of art on the cover. Nor do I care for spiral (wirebound) notebooks; they're difficult to stack or shelve, and their wire spine-ends never fail to snag on something—or gouge into the side of my hand, as I'm a lefty. Glue-backed notebooks aren't good for long-term use because the pages tend to separate easily.

Regardless of the type of daybook you choose, your aim is to pan the steady stream of daily experience for those gold nuggets that can be smelted and fashioned into personal essays. True, while good ideas are everywhere, that does not mean good ideas are conspicuous. While certainly a lot more common than literal gold nuggets, good ideas for lifewriting still need to be sifted carefully from the sand and silt of the everyday.

A Daybook by any other name ...

• *Journal*, from the French word, *jour*, meaning "day"; hence, "journal" and "daybook" are etymologically the same, except that "journal" has come to mean other things, like "periodical" or "newspaper" (thus the word "journalism").

• *Diary*, also from a word meaning "day"—this time Latin (*diem*)— to indicate a daily record of one's thoughts. A diary, unlike a journal, has come to refer to private personal jottings.

• *Log.* This is what you keep when you must maintain an official record of your activities and progress on a project.

• *Notebook.* The most generic of these broadly defined terms, a notebook can incorporate any or all of the above, together with bona fide notes that one takes while reading or listening to lectures or, perhaps, recording the names of plants and animal species encountered while on a nature hike.

How to Keep a Daybook: Three Easy Steps

Writers keep daybooks in order to capture potentially useful thoughts before they vanish forever, but "potentially useful" can mean a lot of things. Who can possibly tell whether a thought of the moment has potential for being developed into an essay? That's one of the adventures of being a writer. Since it isn't practical to write down everything that floods through your mind, you need to trust your intuition and jot down things that have the feel of an insight, or seem like the tip of an iceberg of possibility. Let's say you've been reading a *Dear Abby* column and you come upon a letter in which a mother expresses frustration over not being able to communicate with her teenage daughter. Pay attention to the associations, emotional reactions, ideas, that suddenly flood through your mind. Five minutes' worth of jotting in you daybook might produce the germ of a lifewriting essay—perhaps an entry along these lines:

> Impatient, shortsighted woman! Of course her daughter would react with a temper tantrum. Few things are more important in parent-child relationships than the willingness to communicate. That means not only giving the kid a chance to explain why she wants to take a cross-country road trip with her buddies, but encouraging her to explain. Gosh, I just realized how short-tempered I've been when my son asks me if he can do something I instantly disfavor.

In the above example, the mother reading the *Dear Abby* letter experienced a sudden emotional reaction to the mother who wrote the letter. A non-writer would have let that emotional response fade into oblivion, but this mother instantly sensed that a valuable lesson about parent-child relationships might be captured in a quick daybook-jotting. In the meantime, by being predisposed to turning thoughts into words on paper, you are sharpening your powers of observation, heightening your sense of what could become material for essays.

The first step, then, in keeping a daybook, is *to put yourself in a state of readiness* for recording your thoughts. Overhearing a couple quarrelling, saying mean things to each other, reminds you of a recent argument you've had with your significant other. Suddenly it occurs to you how easily such quarrels and name-calling can be prevented, a possible topic for a lifewriting essay!

A weekend visit to an auto show featuring classic cars magically reawakens childhood memories of your parents' first Packard, or your own very first car, both seeds for a nostalgic essay about those classy old automobiles you wish were still around. The auto show will give you the opportunity to see these vintage models close-up—and to capture them in the daybook you will have wisely brought along just for that occasion.

The second step in keeping a daybook, once you have "primed" yourself to observe and jot down potentially useful material, is actually embedded in the first: *Ask questions about the subject matter* that you might not have asked otherwise. Let's go back to that *Dear Abby* letter about the frustrated mother who can't communicate to her teenage daughter. Think of the questions that might form in your mind about the mother or the daughter—questions like the following:

- Why didn't the mother take more time to see things from her daughter's perspective?
- Why didn't she convey a more compassionate attitude?
- What can I (and other parents) learn from this particular mother-daughter relationship?

And, there is a third step, which needs to be enacted simultaneously with the first two, and that is, *silence the editor in your head* whenever you're writing in your daybook—ignore the nagging voice that keeps telling you to worry about grammar and spelling and mechanics and logical progression of ideas and good sentence and paragraph construction and whatnot when you're simply trying to amass material. The editor in your head doesn't recognize the distinction between daybook jotting and proofreading a final draft.

Using Your Daybook To Maximum Advantage

Okay, you've spent the past several days fattening your daybook with a smorgasbord of observations and ideas and memories. Now what? How do you get from disorganized jottings to coherent drafts of essays? Here are a few tips:

- *Highlight entries that revolve around a similar topic or theme.*
  Simply go through your daybook and, using a red (or any conspicuous color) pen, label the subject matter of each entry with as few words as possible: i.e., auto show; nephew's wedding; fishing trip; home remodeling; people sketches; airport; embarrassing moment; proud moment; list of worries; conversations overheard; quantum-physics lecture. Ideally, you will remember to do this after completing each entry.

- *Review all the marked entries at one sitting and jot down topics that spring to mind.*
  Don't worry yet about committing to a topic. Right now, you simply want to identify potential topics you can see yourself developing into lifewriting features sooner or later.

- *Brainstorm for possibilities.*
  Which of the topics that you jotted down is calling to you the loudest? That is, which topic do you feel most enthusiastic about tackling? Heed that inner voice! If none of the topics seems to stimulate you as much as you think it should, then you can try one or more of the following:

  (a) Devote the next few days to gathering more information or generating more personal reflections about one topic.

  (b) Continue to reflect and gather information about all, or at least a few, of the topics you've identified. Don't be impatient with yourself. Before you can start writing on a topic, you need to feel confident that you have a lot to say about it. Indeed, you should feel that you have more to say about the topic than you could possibly put into a single essay.

Acquiring the Daybook Habit

As with any beneficial habit, you need to allow a certain amount of time for it to take—I suggest allowing two weeks. That is, plan to spend at least two weeks willfully persuading yourself to write in your daybook on a regular basis—at least once a day—before expecting the habit of daybook writing to saturate your neurons to the point where resistance gets transformed into desire. If there is a genuine secret to becoming a writer, it is this: You must find a way to transform the chore of writing into the pleasurable habit of writing.

I once asked the distinguished novelist and essayist Susan Sontag if she had any suggestions for helping students overcome their resistance to writing. She looked bewildered and said that she did not because her problem was never how to begin writing but how to *stop* writing. The implication is that part of what it means to be a writer is to experience both desire and urgency in putting thoughts on paper. Writing then becomes almost as natural as breathing.

Daybook Activities

Most of us, alas, unlike Susan Sontag, need a daily jump-start to get our writing engines fired up. The following exercises are designed to get you into a writing frame of mind, and to get those pages filled. Again, keep in mind that at this stage you're trying to establish habits, and habits require time to establish themselves.

1. Particulars bring writing to life; you need to pay attention to the little things one tends to overlook in casual observations.

So, armed with daybook and pencil or pen, take a tour of your own house and jot down things you've never noticed before—even if you've lived in the same house for many years.

Start with the kitchen. Open a cupboard at random, and on one side of the page list everything that's on the shelves. Everything. Then, on the other side of the page, jot down as much of the *history* of each item as you can recall: when you purchased it, and why; how long it's been sitting there; when you used it last and for what purpose; and, if you wish, list the important things that have happened in your life since it's been there. Remember, unexpected ideas for lifewriting essays lurk everywhere; you may have gotten that bottle of cinnamon sticks to spice up a dessert you fixed for your wife to celebrate her promotion.

The kitchen should keep you busy writing for a week. You can then tour the other rooms in your home, daybook in tow, in much the same way.

2. Use your daybook to help you improve your ability to identify things.

Examples: flowers, trees, types of houses, types of rooftops, types of insects, breeds of dogs and cats, other kinds of wildlife, types of rocks and minerals. You might want to obtain pocket-sized nature guides for some of these. In your daybook record the name and specific location of each specimen you come across, make as detailed a sketch of a leaf or blossom as you can, and cross-reference it with the nature guide. Get in the habit of attaching names to things you would not ordinarily name, such as the particular shape of a particular species of leaf.

3. Use your daybook to record your childhood and adolescent memories.

In fact, you may want to keep a separate daybook exclusively for such memories, dividing it, say, into five sections: Earliest Memories (ages 3–6), Middle Childhood Memories (7–9), Pre-Teen Memories (10–12), Adolescent Years (13–17), and Young Adult Years (18–22). You will discover that the more time you spend writing down early memories, the more memories you will awaken.

4. Use your daybook to record your family's history.

Every family possesses a treasure trove of stories. They are latent in old photographs, in documents and letters, and in oral histories. You most likely know bits and pieces of your family history through casual stories your grandparents, aunts, uncles, and cousins may have shared with you. Prepare questions to ask your relatives in order to fill in gaps in the stories, then use your daybook to create detailed narratives based on these stories.

5. Use your daybook to record the family histories of your friends.

Most people love sharing stories about their families—immediate as well as extended. Ask them to share photographs (always an excellent memory-prompt) as well as stories handed down orally.

6. Begin an open-ended daybook entry devoted to self-assessment.

"Know thyself" is sometimes said to be the beginning of wisdom. Take detailed notes on some or all of the following:

- Your good habits *and* your bad habits
- Deeds, decisions, you are proud of…and those you're ashamed of
- Deepest beliefs, convictions…and your deepest doubts, uncertainties
- "If I could do X over again, here is what I would do…."
- How you think you come across to others, to your children or parents, to your boss, your rivals. How did you manage to cultivate your most valued friendships? On the other hand, what personality clashes, misdeeds, attitudes, beliefs, etc. caused you to have enemies?

Honest self-assessment is not as easy as it may seem, but it is important because it's a natural human tendency to repress our faults and weaknesses and exaggerate our strengths and virtues. But good writing depends on truthful writing. The harder you work at being objective, of acknowledging the bad along with the good in yourself as well as in others, the likelier you are to succeed at lifewriting.

7. Use your daybook as a nightbook.

Take your daybook to bed with you and in that twilight zone between wakefulness and sleep, spill your freethinking onto the page.

You'll be amazed by the strange train of associations that issue forth.

8. Use your daybook to chronicle a long-term project.

You've just begun your first day of training in preparation for running in the Boston Marathon. You've run marathons before, so you know what the competition is like, and what it takes to run competitively in any of them, let alone the most famous of them. But this time, you've come up with a plan you hope will put you among the winners. You've also decided to write an essay about the experience of training for marathons, so you've decided to use your daybook to record the details of your training, including your dietary restrictions, the times of day you begin and end your workouts, the distances you cover, any injuries you experience, setbacks, and of course, the mental preparation involved.

Or consider this scenario: You are a writer who wants to share your skills with young adults—not just any young adults, but those off to a bad start in life, juvenile delinquents, in the hopes that writing could help turn their lives around. This is exactly what novelist Mark Salzman has done. For one year, he taught high-risk young offenders at Central Juvenile Hall in Los Angeles, recorded the experience in his notebooks, and finally published them in book form: *True Notebooks: A Writer's Year at Juvenile Hall* (Knopf, 2003).

9. Use your daybook to create people profiles.

Again, use the same criteria as you used for your self-assessment. This last exercise, undertaken on a regular basis, will yield rich results. Let's take a closer look at how it works.

Using Your Daybook to Create People Profiles

People lie at the heart of lifewriting. Use your daybook for building profiles of the most interesting individuals you know, or have known—teachers, coworkers, family members, friends, people you *dislike*—and yes, you yourself as well. Do not restrict your descriptions only to what is pleasant or positive. People are as memorable for their flaws as for their strengths, and that is what makes them interesting and worth writing about. When doing your people profiling, try to go beyond superficial or cliché attributes (e.g., "rugged tan," "dazzling smile"). Try to capture what is distinctive about your subject—not only his or her appearance, but personality as well. Consider Scott Russell Sanders' description of his alcoholic father in his essay, "Under the Influence":

> In the perennial present of memory, I slip into the garage or barn to see my father tipping back the flat green bottles of wine, the brown cylinders of whiskey, the cans of beer disguised in paper bags. His Adam's apple bobs, the liquid gurgles, he wipes the sandy-haired back of a hand over his lips, and then, his bloodshot gaze bumping into me, he stashes the bottle or can inside his jacket, under the workbench, between two bales of hay, and we both pretend the moment has not occurred.
>
> *Harper's Magazine*; November 1989

In just a couple of sentences, Sanders's father comes to life inside our heads. The trick is to use highly specific details—not just "drinking bottles of wine" but "*tipping back the flat green* bottles of wine"; not just "wipes his lips" but "he wipes the *sandy-haired back of his hand* over his lips."

Here's a people-watching game that I love to play with my wife when we're traveling or out on the town: We conjure up scenarios for persons we observe around us, in a restaurant or bar, in an art gallery, at the airport. If you have your pocket daybook handy, you might compose one-page sketches of individuals or couples you observe. Why is that woman sitting alone at the bar inside the Fairmont Hotel? What is it about her appearance, her expressions, her apparent age, the comments she makes to the bartender, that provides clues? What kind of jewelry is she wearing? Is there a wedding ring? A quick sketch in your pocket notebook could someday provide the spark for an essay on the emotional turmoil of divorced, mid-career, middle-aged women in America.

What to Include in Your People Profiles

You may wish to prepare your profiles in outline or narrative format; either way, try to capture specific details; avoid relying on sweeping generalizations.

- Facial features
- Whole-body descriptions
- Active description (how he or she moves about, gestures)
- Ways of interacting with others
- Manner of speaking
- Special interests, tastes
- Nervous habits, quirks
- Manners, temperament

Additional Fun Things to Do with Your Daybook

Writing is hard work, but hard work needn't exclude having fun. One might even argue that people become successful at what they do when they find a way to combine hard work with pleasure. The following daybook exercises are aimed at emphasizing the fun aspects of writing spontaneously.

1. Your daybook is like a junk drawer in some ways.

You drop things into it spontaneously, without any sense of order or purpose, other than that it *might* be useful someday. In another way, though, it is like one of those chemistry sets you may have gotten for a birthday present when you were a kid. Your daybook entries are the chemicals. What would happen if you combined some of them? Here are a few possibilities:

- An entry describing the contents of a son's or daughter's toy chest + an entry recollecting a fanciful childhood experience of your own = an essay about the way toys have changed from the time of your early childhood to the time of your son's or daughter's childhood.

- An entry about a recent visit to the animal shelter, and how upset you were to see so many abandoned, forlorn cats and dogs + an entry reflecting on the many ways in which dogs and cats bring joy to one's life and one's family = an essay suggesting new publicity strategies your local animal shelter might use to increase the number of adoptions.

2. Take your daybook with you on your next adventure and try capturing "thrill of the moment" experiences, such as the following:

- a ride in a hot-air balloon
- a whale-watching excursion
- a roller-coaster ride (better wait until you get off the roller coaster before you try writing anything down, though!)
- a visit to a sacred or exotic site, or a memorial

Let me share a couple of my own daybook excerpts relating to the last suggestion. During a recent trip to Italy, I recorded my spontaneous reactions to walking down a street in Pompeii, the Roman seacoast town that was rapidly buried under volcanic ash when Mt. Vesuvius erupted in A.D. 79:

> I am walking over the cobblestone streets laid down
> by slaves who lived when Vespasian was Emperor of Rome.
> The ox-cart tracks cut deeply into the stone. Outer walls

of many homes, one with the roof still on, hole in the center for sunlight to pass through. Frescoes still vibrant on walls. Lovely interior atriums…Climb these steps and above the treetops, majestic in the haze, looms Mt. Vesuvius, so unmistakably a volcano with that flat top…Ancient Rome no longer the textbook abstraction it once was. Here I touch the stones, and absorb that long-ago world through my pores.

It is important, you see, to capture not only the details of what you observe, but also your emotional responses to them. Both will need to be fresh in your memory when you get around to writing the essay.

Published Daybooks and Journals

Reading other writers' daybooks reveals the spontaneous thought processes of authors. What we first notice about many of them is their *ordinariness*. With rare exception do we encounter passages of wonderful writing in the daybooks of wonderful writers. What we notice most—and what is most instructive to us—is the writerly mind interacting with the world.

Here is a sampling of published daybooks:

- *Mrs. Thatcher's Minister: The Private Diaries of Alan Clark* by Alan Clark. Scandals, foibles, political scheming—you name it—all appear in these diaries kept by a high-ranking member of parliament under Margaret Thatcher.
- *The Crack-Up* by F. Scott. Fitzgerald. Contains excerpts from his daybooks (what he called his commonplace book). Many entries consist of fragments or single sentences.
- *Diaries* by Franz Kafka. Fascinating descriptions of dreams, strange encounters, feelings of isolation, along with accounts of the social and literary life in pre-war Prague by one of the masters of twentieth century literature.

- *The Journals of Lewis and Clark* by Meriwether Lewis and William Clark. The famous explorers' experiences during their exploration of the vast territory of the Louisiana Purchase and the Pacific Northwest.

- *The Journals of Sylvia Plath* by Sylvia Plath. The eloquent yet often anguished reflections of a major American poet who took her own life when she was thirty years old.

- Salzman, Mark. *True Notebooks: A Writer's Year at Juvenile Hall.* (Discussed above).

- *Journals* by Henry David Thoreau. Thoreau's complete journals, which he used extensively to fashion his books, including *Walden*, comprise fourteen volumes. Several paperback editions of selections from Thoreau's journals exist.

- *Notebooks* by Mark Twain. Very messy and fragmentary. Fun to browse through.

- *The Daybooks of Edward Weston* by Edward Weston. Fascinating reflections and commentary by the world-renowned photographer.

Finally, let me mention a fascinating anthology of daybook excerpts:

- *The Pleasures of Diaries: Four Centuries of Private Writing* edited by Ronald Blythe

Blythe's categories are illuminating: The Diarist as Eye-Witness; the Diarist in Love; the Diarist and the Difficult Marriage; the Diarist in the Village; the Diarist as Naturalist (an excerpt from Charles Darwin's diary is included); the Sick Diarist (diary excerpts from the short story writer Katherine Mansfield and others); the Diarist in the Shop; the Diarist at War (including a diary excerpt by Evelyn Waugh); the Diarist as Artist (excerpts from the diaries of Dorothy Wordsworth, the great poet's sister, Gerard Manley Hopkins, Virginia Woolf, Anais Nin): Diaries and Royalty; the Diarist en Route; the Diarist in Despair; the Diarist and Death.

3

Digging for Information

In this Chapter
~ Starting with what you already know
~ Acquiring a nose for you need to know
~ Sleuthing for information: where to begin?
~ Navigating the Internet
~ Interviewing: from the horse's mouth

Writers are curiosity-driven folks. Curiosity is an important attribute because it motivates us to ask questions about things we don't understand. The higher our level of curiosity, the more questions we ask, and the more we learn.

But asking questions is one thing, knowing where to go for answers—the most thorough and reliable answers—is another. This chapter will guide you through the jungle of information resources out there, but before embarking on a research safari, you need to have at least a general idea of the kind of information you're looking for.

Starting with What You Already Know

The first step in gathering information might surprise you: It's to take stock of what you yourself already know about the topic at hand. The reason for this is quite simple, because you most likely know more about the topic than you realize. Bits of information and memories not immediately useful to us get stored away—archived, you might say—in our memories. To get at them again you need to perform specific retrieval tasks. Your daybook will come in handy for retrieving this dormant knowledge.

Spend a day or two recording everything you know about the topic you'd like to write about. You might also begin a concurrent entry, "What I Need to Know about X," although much of this may not come to mind until you actually begin work on the draft itself. I suggest you prepare both of these entries in list form to make them easy to reference when you begin the outlining or drafting. If you want to write about your uncle's experiences as a helicopter pilot during the Vietnam War, you might make a "need to know" list that looks something like this:

What I Need to Know About Uncle Gilbert's Experiences as a Helicopter Pilot in Vietnam:

- What were his duties as a chopper pilot?
- What was his most dangerous mission?
- What was a typical flying mission like?
- Where in Vietnam did his missions take him?
- How often did he fly?
- What insights into the conflict did his perspective as a pilot give him?

As you might guess, these preliminary jottings will help prepare you for an interview with your uncle.

Acquiring a Nose for What You Need to Know

Writers sometimes get caricatured as ivory-tower types, sequestered from the world, living only in their imaginations. Not true—not even for fiction writers (who almost always must do research to make their stories and characters and settings seem credible). If you want to be a writer, you need to get out in the world, not only to become deeply familiar with the things that interest you, but to interact with people who engage in these areas of interest—machinists, business executives, lawyers, farmers, teachers, military officers, scientists, athletes, you name it.

Let's say that one of your neighbors is an amateur astronomer. Often, on clear nights, you'll see her out on her patio gazing through a telescope. Let's also say that you're curious about what makes stargazing so fascinating. Beyond enjoying the romantic associations that a full moon triggers now and then, you've never given the night sky much thought; in fact, you've always associated stargazing with childhood daydreaming, with Tinker Bell and stardust—too disconnected from real life for your taste.

One day, you share your sentiments with your stargazing neighbor, and she gives you an earful: "The universe has a lot to do with real life," she says. "The Earth and everything on it, including ourselves, is made of stuff that was cooked inside of stars billions of years ago. The stars blew up, scattered their heavier elements—carbon and iron and phosphorus— the elements essential for life—into space, and voila! here we are. That makes us literally a part of the heavens."

Being the nose-for-news kind of person that you are, you sense an idea for a lifewriting feature starting to brew. You run back indoors to grab your daybook, then return for more.

Your amateur astronomer neighbor continues to share her knowledge of and enthusiasm for her hobby. Titles start streaming through your head: "How Stargazing Can Improve Your Life"; "Astronomy, Not Astrology, Can Shape Your Destiny"; "Seeing Stars: A Guide for Lovers." But before you can zip out a draft or even an outline or treatment of such a piece, you need to learn more about stars and planets, and telescopes.

First, begin a list of what you already know about astronomy. The list might look something like this:

- The names of planets and constellations (e.g., Mercury, Venus; Orion, Gemini, Cassiopeia) come from Greek mythology, suggesting a link between pagan religious belief and astronomy

- Stars are suns like our own, but incredibly distant—that's why they don't appear to shift positions relative to each other, not even over several centuries

- There are several different types of stars, from tiny earth-size "white dwarfs" to "supergiants"—stars thousands of times larger than our sun

- What we call "the solar system" consists not only of the sun and planets and moons that revolve around planets, but also comets and asteroids (most of these forming a belt between the orbits of Mars and Jupiter)

- Speaking of asteroids: Many have not been discovered; some have eccentric orbits, and a few of these actually cross earth's orbit—and that means there's a remote chance of collision.... An asteroid collision is what was supposed to have killed off the dinosaurs and was the basis for two recent science fiction movies, Armageddon and Deep Impact

- Some famous astronomers: Edwin Hubble (after whom the Hubble Space Telescope was named), was the first to show that the universe was expanding and that some of the "nebulae" (i.e., interstellar gas clouds) were actually distant galaxies; Percival Lowell, a late-nineteenth-century astronomer who thought that there were canals (hence intelligent life) on Mars; and, of course, Galileo, who first used a telescope for astronomical purposes, discovering that Venus had phases and that Jupiter had moons

"Hmm, not bad," you say to yourself, looking over your brain-dump; "I had no idea I knew all that!"

Another possible preliminary step, assuming you have the time, is to enroll in an extension course on astronomy at your local college. Doing so will provide you with in-depth knowledge, possibly give you an opportunity to observe celestial phenomena firsthand through a large telescope, and provide access to at least one other expert in the field: your instructor.

Sleuthing for Information: Where to Begin?

Once you have at least a glimmering of the gaps in your knowledge-base, it's time to pay a visit to your local public or college library. A quick note about college libraries: If you are not enrolled as a student there, you will often need to apply for a visitor's card and pay a fee—usually well worth it, though, because the resources of college libraries are often greater than those of local public libraries. Exceptions are the public libraries in major cities like New York and Boston, which have holdings as great as those of the best universities. As I write, the newly rebuilt San Jose Public Library in San Jose, California, has just opened, combining the resources of the old SJPL with those of San Jose State University (whose campus is a few blocks away)—the first library of its kind in the United States. If it proves successful, this type of library could become widespread.

The largest public library of all is the Library of Congress in Washington, DC, with its 100 million books and periodicals, occupying more than 500 miles of shelving. You can access the electronic catalogues of some libraries off-site via the Internet. Want to browse the Library of Congress catalogue? Just go to <www.loc.gov>

Internet access is enormously practical and a great convenience—but nothing can replace an actual visit to a library, where you can browse through real books and periodicals. Your first stop will be the reference section. Here is where you find the encyclopedias, indexes, abstracts, bibliographies, maps, concordances, dictionaries, and handbooks. These are foundational reference works in the sense that they cover the basics and lead you to other books, articles, and media resources.

Navigating the Internet

Thanks to the Internet, virtually any information you need is literally at your fingertips, via your computer keyboard. As little as fifteen years ago, what you couldn't learn by telephone or direct personal contact, you had to look up in books and periodicals at your local (or not-so-local) library. Libraries continue to be necessary, of course, particularly for in-depth research. Even in the future when it will be possible to call up virtually any book or document on your computer screen, print books will continue to prove their worth; they are just too handy to read and browse to be completely replaced.

Research Tools and Resources

Internet A cyber-universe in which virtually any topic can be surveyed. Ideal for background information rather than in-depth information. Web sites relating to a given topic may be called up with keyword searches, via a search engine such as Google [www.google.com] or Yahoo [www.yahoo.com]

General encyclopedias Quick background information; bibliography often accompanies major articles. Some encyclopedias, such as *Encyclopedia Britannica* or *Encarta*, are available online or on CD-ROM.

Specialized encylopedias Encyclopedias that include articles on subjects relating to just one knowledge domain or subject area, e.g., *The McGraw-Hill Encyclopedia of Science and Technology*; *The Encyclopedia of Philosophy*.

Dictionaries Like encyclopedias, dictionaries can be general or specialized. Specialized dictionaries exist for virtually every subject. The most important unabridged dictionary in English is the monumental *Oxford English Dictionary*, in 24 folio-sized volumes. What makes it so huge? The usage history, with examples, of nearly every word in the language is presented.

Directories These workhorse publications list the names and addresses of service providers, together with descriptions of services provided. An important directory for writers is *Literary Market Place*, which lists names and addresses of bona fide literary agents, book and periodical publishers, and editorial contacts. *The American Directory of Writer's Guidelines* is useful for finding in-depth information on what individual publishers are looking for. It is also a good place to browse for lifewriting ideas.

Concordances Need to know what the Bible specifically has to say about bread, both literally and metaphorically? Or, how often any particular other word appears in the Bible? Then a Bible concordance is what you need. A concordance is a list, arranged alphabetically, of every word used in a given work or by a given author. Some concordances, provide the sentences or verse passages in which in each word appears. *Young's Analytical Concordance to the Bible*, for example, includes 311,000 separate quotations and references. There are concordances to Shakespeare, to Emily Dickinson, and many other major authors.

Maps Most of us are quite familiar with *road maps*, what we turn to to find our way around a city or state, but many other kinds of maps exist, such as *geological maps*, used to describe bedrock and natural-resource formations in a given region; *topographical maps*, that depict mountain ranges; *geographical maps* that indicate bioregions such as farmland, forest, desert, marshland, and so on; *historical maps* that depict political boundaries of cities, states, empires during a given period.

Government documents The United States government is the largest publisher in the country, producing many thousands of documents, written by and for the hundreds of federal agencies such as NASA, the EPA, the Bureau of Weights and Measures, the Department of the Interior, the National Wildlife Association, the FTC, and so on. Most libraries have a government documents section.

Indexes These references enable you to locate articles published in periodicals—newspapers, magazines, professional journals—in a given year. Articles are indexed by title as well as by author. Examples: *Health Sciences Index, Education Index.*

Experts Individuals with professional knowledge of or first-hand experience with the subject in question. Just about everyone is an expert in some area (the area of one's livelihood). When doing library research, pay a visit to the experts *there*—the librarians. Assisting patrons is part of their job, so don't hesitate to take advantage of their services.

An Internet search engine is an ideal place to begin your Web search. You're probably already familiar with the best known engines: Google <www.google.com> and Yahoo <www.yahoo.com>. Type in a name, a topic, a keyword, and the search engine will bring up hundreds, even thousands of hits—which is a mixed blessing, because a lot of those hits will be off the mark or altogether irrelevant. If you enter specific terms, chances are the first hits will prove to be the most relevant.

Another thing to keep in mind when researching on the Internet is that there's a lot of junk out there. Oh sure, there's junk in libraries, too, but part of librarians' jobs is to weed out junk. Any charlatan or crackpot can post information on the Web, and, alas, there are no cyber-librarians to separate the wheat from the chaff—that is a task each of us must learn to do on our own.

Allow me to suggest the following three pointers for helping you identify what is reputable from what is not:

1. Check the credentials of authors whose articles you access on the Web. Simply enter the names in Google or Yahoo and see what comes up. Look for education, training, professional experience, previous publications.

2. Make sure that information from a given Web site is not biased, politically partisan, or sponsored by a profit-making organization. For example, if you're doing research on Charles Darwin, you probably would not want to rely on information obtained from a site affiliated with creationists. Nor would you be likely to find unbiased information located about the hazards of tobacco on a Web site sponsored by a cigarette manufacturer.

3. Test the validity of the information by running cross-checks, not just with information on other Web sites, but from books and articles.

Interviewing: From the Horse's Mouth

The information you obtain from the Internet or from books, periodicals, and other kinds of documents in the library is known collectively as *secondary* source material—secondary because you are reading works whose factual content was researched by their respective authors. But equally important is *primary* source material: data obtained from your own field or laboratory work, or the field and lab work of others; unpublished speeches and lectures; legal or other forms of testimony; unpublished logs, diaries, notebooks; accumulated, unprocessed ("raw") data, and interviews—formal or informal.

Interviewing is a wonderfully efficient method of information gathering—and for lifewriting projects, the interviewees themselves, as much as the information they provide, will be of interest to readers.

Think of an interview as a conversation with a person who has important information to share with you, or whose life story is, or could be, of great interest to many readers. The best kind of interview is one in which the interviewee feels at ease and is able to exhibit something of his or her personality. This may take some advance preparation on your part, because people, especially celebrities, may well have had negative experiences with interviewers, so you'll want to keep the following in mind:

- Schedule your interview well in advance; most people worth interviewing have tight schedules

- Decide on the specific purpose of the interview, and communicate that purpose clearly to the interviewee. Avoid vague or grandiose goals, such "I'd like to write about the secret of your success." Instead, limit yourself to something manageable, such as "I'd like to write about the steps you took to create your program for the homeless"

- Make your interview a conversation, not an interrogation. Arrive with a prepared set of questions, but don't rely exclusively on them. That is, expect to ask what I like to call "spin-off questions"—questions that occur to you spontaneously in reaction to the way the person you're interviewing responds to a prepared question

- Always thank the interviewee for his or her time, and ask permission to follow up with additional questions (via phone or e-mail) later

- Prepare a transcript of your interview immediately, even if you've taped it. Doing so will help you think of possible follow-up questions.

EXERCISES

1. Locate five different biographies of Martin Luther King, Jr. on the Internet. Next, determine which ones seem most reliable and which least reliable. What led you to make those determinations?

2. Conduct an interview with someone in your workplace or educational institution who is knowledgeable about the company's or institution's history. Focus the interview on one specific period, such as its founding.

3. Over the next few days, surprise yourself with how much you know about a given topic by preparing "What I Know about X" entries in you daybook. Here are some possibilities:

What I already know about...

- Parenting challenges
- Hosting a dinner party—what works, what doesn't
- The art of reconciliation (with a parent, a child, a sibling, a spouse, a neighbor)
- Therapy (physical or psychological)
- Starting a new job
- Good study habits
- Collecting Coca-Cola memorabilia

_4_

Transforming Raw Data into Lifewriting: Key Techniques to Master

In this Chapter
~ Four basic techniques of lifewriting
~ Show, don't tell, or how to create dramatic immediacy
~ Bringing in the particulars, or details, details, _details_
~ Narrate along a "rising curve" of expectation
~ Project your natural voice

If you've been filling your daybook with ideas and observations during the last few weeks, you may already have accumulated enough raw material to launch several lifewriting features. However, eager as you might be to get those features written, you need to be sure that you have a solid grasp of basic techniques.

Four Basic Techniques of Lifewriting

Lifewriting, like fiction, is most successful when it engages the reader's interest and emotions. Use the following techniques to accomplish this:

1. Create dramatic immediacy; that is, *show* more than *tell*.

2. Favor concrete details over abstract generalizations.

3. Generate curiosity about what will happen next, or be re-vealed next, by narrating along a "rising curve" of expectation.

4. Put yourself in the piece, not just with the first person point of view, but through your voice.

A fifth technique, structuring the writing project, will be discussed in Chapters 5 and 6.

Show, Don't Tell, or How to Create Dramatic Immediacy

Three writers are sitting in the local park, watching children frolicking on the monkey bars and slides. The kids seem to be having a fine time role-playing, coming up with different stunts, shrieking with excitement. Writer A opens his daybook and starts to scribble:

> This afternoon I notice that several neighborhood chil-dren are having lots of fun in the park. Some like to play on the monkey bars while others prefer the slide or the jungle-gym. The children are all such bundles of energy.
>
> Any adult who watches children at play like this is bound to feel nostalgic for the days when he was a child.

Writer A pauses to reread the passage. As a daybook entry, it serves the purpose of capturing a moment that could trigger a lifewriting essay in the future. But suppose Writer A is thinking about using the entry "as is" in an essay. Does it pass muster? Well, it's clear and grammatical, but it does not engage the reader's interest. Why not? Lack of concrete, sensory de-tails (which we'll concern ourselves with next) is part of the reason, but not the only one. Mainly, it's because the writer only summarizes what he saw; he does not *dramatize* it.

To dramatize a scene, you need to introduce a sense of immediacy—convey the impression that the scene is unfolding before the reader's eyes in the present moment, the way a scene is enacted on the stage or screen.

Now let's look over Writer B's shoulder:

> Several neighborhood boys and girls like to propel themselves across the monkey bars or leap through space on the swings and slides. It can make an onlooker dizzy. Who can watch such mayhem without feeling a nostalgic tug in the loins, a desire to leap into the fray with those shrieking children, and to become a child again?

Hmmm, that seems a little bit livelier. A little more expressive. Unlike the first paragraph, we can sense the writer's presence (more about that when we get to the last step), but something is still missing. Do you see what it is? A peek at what Writer C has written should give you the answer quickly:

> The freckled redhead with pigtails seems to be the ringleader—or maybe "jungle banshee" would be a more appropriate name for her—uttering her war cry as she flings herself in a graceful arc off the parallel bars and smack onto the midst of her fellow urchins.
> "Yeeeew!" one of the urchins screeches. "Spider Woman just landed on me!"
> There, I think to myself, are the perfect examples of the wild child I'd always secretly wanted to be.

Writer C brings the scene to life by focusing on individual children, and by rendering the moment as present action. Readers are drawn into a story in the process of unfolding, rather than presented with a static summary of a past action. Writer C doesn't just tell us that the children are frolicking, she dramatizes it through action words and dialogue.

Bringing in the Particulars, or Details, Details, *Details*!

A close cousin to the technique of dramatization is that of detailed description. You want to describe a scene in a way that enables readers to experience it vicariously—as if *they* were the ones observing it. Which of the following descriptions of the same scene best engages your attention?

(a) I know well a stretch of road where nature's own landscaping has provided a border of different species of trees and flowers, with colors that change with the seasons.

(b) I know well a stretch of road where nature's own landscaping has provided a border of alder, viburnum, sweet fern, and juniper, with seasonally changing accents of bright flowers or of fruits hanging in jeweled clusters in the fall.

My guess is that you found sentence (b) more engaging because of the use of particular details rather than the broad generalizations of sentence (a). Particular details stimulate one or more of the senses (in this

Summarizing vs. Showing

Compare the summary-like passage in example (a) to its dramatized counterpart in example (b). *Showing* what happens holds the reader's attention more securely than merely summarizing what happens.

(a) I remember that hiking in the mountain was difficult, and there were many moments when I thought I would pass out from exhaustion or lose my balance and slip into the gorge.

(b) My lungs were heaving now as I forced one foot in front of the other. The sun kept beating relentlessly against my neck, making me dizzy. I began to slip off the trail. "Watch out!" Larry exclaimed. If the dizziness continued, I would be in trouble.

case the sense of sight; we can visualize the floral beauty bordering the road). The vivid imagery also gives us a keener sense of the narrator's presence. By the way, the author of that second version is Rachel Carson, from her classic work, *Silent Spring*.

Narrate Along a "Rising Curve" of Expectation

Narration is, quite simply, a story unfolding. But, you wonder, what does story have to do with lifewriting? Isn't story the realm of fiction rather than nonfiction? Not at all. Stories may be true (nonfiction, essay, lifewriting), or imagined (fiction; epic and narrative poetry). In either case, the writer aims to bring the reader into the story—and the best way to do that is through generating a sense of story buildup—or, if you want a fancier term, narrative progression. We can illustrate this with a simple diagram:

```
                        X
                    X
                X
            X
    X   X   X
```

In the following excerpt from his essay, "Notes of a Native Son," the African-American novelist and playwright James Baldwin dramatizes the moment when, having reached his final point of intolerance against white America's discrimination against blacks, he walks into a café that had a policy of not serving "Negroes":

> I do not know how long I waited .... I hated her for her white face, and for her great, astounded, frightened eyes. I felt that if she found a black man so frightening I would make her fright worthwhile.
>
> She did not ask me what I wanted, but repeated, as though she had learned it somewhere, "We don't serve Negroes here." She did not say it with the blunt, derisive hostility to which I had grown so accustomed, but, rather,

with a note of apology in her voice, and fear. This made me colder and more murderous than ever. I felt I had to do something with my hands. I wanted her to come close enough for me to get her neck between my hands.

Project Your Natural Voice

"Voice" is always a tricky subject to discuss in terms of writing. The word conventionally refers to spoken words, but what exactly does voice mean in the context of writing? For one thing, it refers to the way you like to describe things, your use of favorite expressions or metaphors, the way you like to emphasize an idea. For example, if you are writing about a surfing experience, you might want to emphasize your growing impatience at standing around and waiting for a good wave:

- After nearly an hour of waiting, or catching waves that were little more than swells, I was growing bored and restless— but when the big wave finally came, my heart leaped into my throat, and suddenly I knew why I loved this sport so much ....

But another writer might want to focus less on the waiting and more on the moment when the hoped-for wave finally arrives:

- First one midget wave, then another, then another. I was quickly becoming impatient. But then, without notice, the sea suddenly reared itself up like some giant beast ....

Use your daybook to try out different voices. Try projecting a contemplative voice; an excited voice; a voice in which you wish to communicate a sense of outrage without losing a sense of dignity; a witty, playful, or gently satirical voice.

Playfulness and wit appeal to many readers. As you read the following jab at obnoxious airplane passengers, ask yourself what Pulitzer-prize winning humorist Dave Barry does to create his satiric voice:

Hell On Wings

I'm in an airplane, strapped into my seat, no way to escape. For an hour we've been taxiing around Miami International Airport while lightning tries to hit us. Earlier I was hoping that the plane might at some point actually take off and fly to our intended destination, but now I'm starting to root for the lightning, because a direct strike might silence the two women sitting in front of me. There's only one empty seat between them, but they're speaking at a decibel level that would be appropriate if one of them were in Cleveland. Also, they both have Blitherers Disease, which occurs when there is no filter attached to the brain, so that every thought the victim has, no matter how minor, comes blurting right out. This means that the rest of us passengers are being treated to repartee such as this:

First Woman: I PREFER A WINDOW SEAT.

Second Woman: OH, NOT ME. I ALWAYS PREFER AN AISLE SEAT.

First Woman: THAT'S JUST LIKE MY SON. HE LIVES IN NEW JERSEY, AND HE ALWAYS PREFERS AN AISLE SEAT ALSO.

Second Woman: MY SISTER-IN-LAW WORKS FOR A DENTIST IN NEW JERSEY. HE'S AN EXCELLENT DENTIST BUT HE CAN'T PRONOUNCE HIS R'S. HE SAYS, "I'M AFWAID YOU NEED A WOOT CANAL."

First Woman: MY BROTHER-IN-LAW JUST HAD THAT ROOT CANAL. HE WAS BLEEDING ALL OVER HIS NEW CAR, ONE OF THOSE JAPANESE ONES, A WHADDAYACALLEM, LEXIT.

Second Woman: I PREFER A BUICK, BUT LET ME TELL YOU, THIS INSURANCE, WHO CAN AFFORD IT?

First Woman: I HAVE A BROTHER IN THE INSURANCE BUSINESS, WITH ANGINA. HE PREFERS A WINDOW SEAT.

Second Woman: OH, NOT ME. I ALWAYS PREFER AN AISLE. NOW MY DAUGHTER....

And so it has gone, for one solid hour, a live broadcast of random neural firings. The harder I try to ignore it, the more my brain focuses on it. But it could be worse. I could be the flight attendant. Every time she walks past the two women, they both shout "MISS?" It's an uncontrollable reflex.

"MISS?" they are shouting. "CAN WE GET A BEVERAGE HERE?" This is maybe the fifth time they have asked this.

"I'm sorry," says the flight attendant, with incredible patience. "We can't serve any beverages until after we take off."

The answer never satisfies the women, who do not seem to be fully aware of the fact that the plane is still on the ground. They've decided that the flight attendant has a bad attitude. As she moves away, they discuss this in what they apparently believe is a whisper.

"SHE'S VERY RUDE," they say, their voices booming through the cabin, possibly audible in other planes. "THEY SHOULD FIRE HER." "YES, THEY SHOULD." "THERE'S SUPPOSED TO BE BEVERAGE SERVICE." "MISS?"

It's a good thing for society in general that I'm not a flight attendant, because I would definitely kill somebody no later than my second day. Recently, I sat on a bumpy, crowded flight and watched a 40-ish flight attendant, both arms occupied with a large stack of used dinner trays, struggling down the aisle, trying to maintain her balance, and a young man held out his coffee cup, *blocking her path*, and in a loud, irritated voice said, quote: "Hon? Can I get a refill? Like maybe today?"

Hon.

She smiled—not with her eyes—and said, "I'll be with you as soon as I can, sir."

Sir.

Oh, I'd be with him soon, all right. I'd come up behind him and strangle him with the movie-headphone cord. "Is that tight enough for you, *sir*?" would be the last words he'd ever hear. Then I'd become a legendary outlaw flight attendant. I'd hide in the overhead luggage compartment and watch for problems, such as people flying with small children and making no effort to control them, people who think it's *cute* when their children shriek and pour salad dressing onto other passengers. When this happened BANG the luggage compartment would burst open and out would leap: the Avenging Flight Attendant of Doom, his secret identity concealed by a mask made from a barf bag with holes in it. He'd snatch the child and say to the parents, very politely, "I'm sorry, but FAA regulations require me to have this child raised by somebody more civilized, such as wolves." If they tried to stop him, he'd pin them in their seats with dense, 200-pound airline omelets.

Insane? Yes, I'm insane, and you would be too, if you were listening to these two women.

"MISS??" they are saying. "IT'S TOO HOT IN HERE." "CAN WE GET SOME BEVERAGE SERVICE?" "MISS???"

And now the pilot is making an announcement. "Well, folks" is how he starts. This is a bad sign. They always start with "Well, folks" when they're going to announce something bad, as in: "Well, folks, if we dump the fuel, we might be able to glide as far as the mainland."

This time the pilot announces that—I swear I am not making this up—lightning has struck the control tower.

"We could be sitting here for some time," he says.

"MISS????" say the women in front of me.

No problem. I can handle it. I'll just stay calm, reach into the seat pocket, very slowly pull out the headphone cord …

Dave Barry, "Hell On Wheels," from *Dave Barry Is Not Making This Up*. New York: Crown, 1995.

Even though Barry clearly sets out to get laughs, and uses the time-worn technique of hyperbole in nearly every paragraph, he nonetheless gives a natural, conversational flavor to the piece by using colloquial speech and by modulating his sentence patterns and lengths (something I'll call your attention to again when we discuss ways of developing your writing style in Chapter 8). This combination of exaggeration and conversational normalcy—together with dramatic immediacy—calls attention to the underlying seriousness of the humor, as in this passage:

> Recently, I sat on a bumpy crowded flight and watched a 40-ish flight attendant, both arms occupied with a large stack of used dinner trays, struggling down the aisle, trying to maintain her balance, and a young man held out his coffee cup, *blocking her path*, and in a loud, irritated voice said, quote: "Hon? Can I get a refill? Like maybe today?"
>
> *Hon.*
>
> She smiled—not with her eyes—and said, "I'll be with you as soon as I can, sir."
>
> *Sir.*
>
> Oh, I'd be with him soon all right....

It isn't just laughs for the sake of laughs. People who are discourteous, loudmouths and who are insensitive to the feelings of others (think of those who jabber into their cell phones at the top of their lungs on crowded trains and buses), constitute a genuine social problem. Humor, handled with skill, can be an effective way of dealing with problems.

EXERCISES

1. Strengthen the descriptive power of the following passages by replacing or supplementing the general references (in bold face) with concrete particulars:

(a) The **pieces of furniture** in the antebellum plantation home were **unusual**.

(b) Eddie tripped over **some obstacle** in the field and **hurt himself**. When he got back onto his feet, he started **walking abnormally**.

(c) I planted **several species of flowers** in my garden. My favorites were the **ones with the large blossoms**.

(d) After the party guests left, the living room resembled **a war zone**.

2. Rewrite the following bland sentences so that they take on the characteristics of your own natural voice—using favorite patterns of description or emphasis:

(a) Fishing in the river was good; we must have caught a dozen trout.

(b) People started running out of the building when the fire alarm sounded.

(c) The children seemed to have a fun time riding the roller coaster.

5

Organizing Techniques I:
Working Up an Outline

In this Chapter
~ Making outlines work for you
~ Scratch vs. detailed outlines
~ The role of titles in outlining
~ Constructing the detailed outline
~ Subordinate points, examples, and all that jazz
~ Testing your outline

Does the mere mention of the word *outline* conjure up bleak memories of certain high school or junior high English classes, when your enthusiasm for writing was right up there with tooth extraction? In one of my junior high English classes, the teacher did not permit me to proceed with my assigned essay until she approved of my outline. We were called up to her desk, one by one, and had to stand there attentively while she perused the outline, red pen in hand, jaw clamped. It wasn't enough to present her with a good idea broken down into subtopics—oh no, we had to follow Precise Outline Format (indicating main headings with uppercase Roman numerals, capital letters for subtopics, Arabic numerals for examples—plus we had to articulate each point in complete sentences. And, outline approval was only half the battle; we then had to follow our outlines *to the letter* as we mechanically assembled our five-paragraph themes.

Such a militant approach to outlines (and to writing) defeats the very purpose of this valuable writer's tool. It surprises me to this day that I continued to like writing after that experience.

Making Outlines Work for You

Writing an essay, let alone a book, requires careful planning: what to say and when to say it; what to include and where to include it; how to sustain reader interest; presenting ideas and assertions clearly and convincingly; and so on. But "planning" can refer to different kinds of strategies. Some writers prefer to plunge directly into a first draft and see what comes out, rather than work from outlines. In other words, they prefer to rely on pure intuition and proceed by trial-and-error. If that sounds like you, then more power to you! But outlining does not have to interfere with intuition or spontaneity. An outline will simply help you produce a draft with greater efficiency, because, in essence, it provides you with an instantaneous glimpse of your essay's overall structure so that you can follow it or change it as you see fit.

Let me stress the words "or change it as you see fit." Outlining means *attempting* to establish an organizational scheme for the intended essay, not turning it into a legal contract. You won't know if it works until you try it out. Quite likely, you will rework and fine-tune your outline several times. The longer your project, the more useful an outline will be in helping you visualize which points you want to make and where in the essay (or book) you need to make them. Thus, rather than feel constrained by your outline, you will feel yourself being guided by it.

Let me tell you something else about outlines: They can help you generate content, not just organize it. The effort to put things in order will trigger ideas for the things to put in order. The brain often works in mysterious ways.

Scratch vs. Detailed Outlines

A scratch outline is a spontaneous organizational scheme that you scribble out in a minute or two. Writers often produce scratch outlines when they first think of an idea; that's why it makes sense to keep a pocket notebook available at all times. A scratch outline often will preserve the gut feeling about your topic, so I advise you not to delay in scribbling *something* down right away. Don't worry about ranking your assertions in order of importance at this stage; that will come later. The following prompts are all you need to produce a useful scratch outline:

- What's my working title?
- What do I want this piece to be about? (premise)
- What three or four key points do I want to make about my main idea?

Let's say you're thinking about turning the interview with your amateur astronomer neighbor into a lifewriting feature. You might scribble out a scratch outline that looks something like the following:

> Working Title: "The Family That Gazes Together Stays Together"
>
> Premise: Adding stargazing to one's routine can enrich family life.
>
> > Assertion 1: Amateur astronomy is a relatively inexpensive pursuit, and is easy to get started.
> >
> > Assertion 2: Backyard astronomy is an emotionally and intellectually satisfying way to bring family and friends together.
> >
> > Assertion 3: My neighbor's particular take on the hobby is refreshing.
> >
> > Assertion 4: Telescope-viewing projects are many.

If more specific details occur to you as you plan the framework of the piece, then jot those down too. No sense holding yourself back when ideas are mushrooming like crazy. On the other hand, do one thing at a time, if that makes you more comfortable. It's never any good to feel rushed when planning a writing project.

The Role of Titles in Outlining

In Chapter 1, I talked about the way titles serve as instant curiosity stimulators—after all, the title of your essay is the first thing readers will see. Titles also serve an important purpose when you're organizing your essay. I sometimes annoy my students by repeatedly urging them to come up with a good title early on, no matter if they haven't fully thought out their topics. I might even qualify that by adding, *especially* if they haven't fully thought out their topics. Some writers actually *begin* with a title. A good title—one that at least infers the premise of your feature—can serve as a steady beacon to keep you from straying from your main idea as you plan your feature, which is why it's a good idea to start thinking about possible titles very early on.

An effective title will capture the essence of your feature in as few words as possible—and, if possible, be fresh and clever without being gimmicky. Unless you prove to be a natural at coming up with good titles, don't settle for the first one that comes to mind—likelier than not it will either be dull or over-determined. Remember that if your feature were to be published in a magazine, the title would be the first thing readers would see. Which of the following titles for an essay on a visit to Stonehenge would most pique your curiosity?

- Stonehenge
- My Visit to Stonehenge
- Nirvana amid the Unworldly Druidic Pillars
- The Sacred Stones of Salisbury
- Stonehenge: Lifting the Veils of Mystery

The first two titles are dull; they evince a ho-hum attitude in readers—not good if you don't want to lose readers before they even begin reading your essay! The third title seems forced and doesn't really convey the topic: Not many potential readers will know that "Unworldly Druidic

Pillars" is a reference to Stonehenge. The fourth title is not as pretentious, and does pique curiosity—but the word "sacred" can be misleading in the context of a feature about a pagan structure. The last title, while probably not the best possible title one could conjure up, achieves the dual purpose of conveying the topic and piquing curiosity. Everyone likes to explore a mystery.

Constructing the Detailed Outline

The frame of a detailed (or formal) outline looks much like your scratch outline: Underneath your working title, you state the premise, followed by the major points (or, in the case of a narrative, the key stages of the experience you're relating).

Working title

Premise

First main heading

Second main heading

Third main heading…

…and so on, for as many main headings (components of your premise) as you need. If you want to use Roman numerals and capital letters for subdivision, fine, but that kind of formatting, if you ask me, is a mere carryover from rule-obsessed schoolmarms.

Let's return to your planned piece on the delights and benefits of patio-deck astronomy. Now is the time to start thinking about how you want to rank-order the points you want to make. After mulling over possibilities, settle (at least for the moment) on this arrangement:

Working Title: "The Family That Gazes Together Stays Together"
Premise: Adding stargazing to one's routine can enrich family life.

Amateur astronomy is an emotionally and intellectually satisfying way to bring family and friends together.

Amateur astronomy is an easy and relatively inexpensive pursuit.

There are numerous telescope-viewing opportunities (given the time of year).

My neighbor's particular "take" on the hobby is refreshing.

Subordinate Points, Examples, and All That Jazz

Once your main headings are in place, you can direct your attention to the subordinate points you want to make for each heading:

Main heading
First Point

Second Point

+ example

+ example

Third point …

… and so on

Applying this template to the amateur astronomy piece will produce something like the following:

Amateur astronomy is an emotionally and intellectually satisfying way to bring family and friends together.

The sense of awe and wonder telescopic observations generate in children can quickly translate into scientific curiosity and love of learning in general

The parent-child bonding that results can have far-reaching effects.

It gives children a deeper appreciation for what "parental authority" can entail.

Parents become exemplars for learning, which then transfers over to schoolteachers.

Testing Your Outline

Your outline will keep changing as you continue thinking about your lifewriting topic, especially when you start working on the treatment, and even when you begin the first draft. For that reason, it's a good idea to test your outline occasionally to make sure it reflects the way you want your feature to come together. The following questions will help keep you on track:

1. Do all my main ideas relate directly to and illuminate my premise?

2. Have I arranged the main ideas in the most logical, effective sequence possible for my intentions? Would the feature be more effective if I reorganized the sequence?

3. Have I included all the subordinate points I need for each main idea?

EXERCISES

1. Prepare scratch outlines for one or more of the following topics:

(a) Teaching a child to swim (or to ride a bike)

(b) Moving into a new home

(c) Traveling abroad with young children

(d) Hosting the perfect party: do's and don'ts

(e) The pleasures (and pains) of maintaining a diet (or exercise regimen)

(f) Growing up in _____

2. Come up with at least two curiosity-generating working titles for each of the two scratch outlines you've created

3. Choose one of the scratch outlines you prepared for exercise number 1 and develop it into a more detailed outline

6

Organizing Techniques II:
Writing the Treatment

In this Chapter
~ What is a treatment?
~ Writing the treatment
~ Two kinds of treatments
~ Using a treatment productively

We are getting close to the Main Event—the actual drafting of your lifewriting feature. To ensure that your draft will come together coherently, with minimal difficulty, I strongly recommend preparing a treatment in addition to an outline. Treatments are also referred to as "discovery drafts"—the equivalent of "studies" that artists use to describe the quick painting of a scene on paper prior to a full rendering of it on canvas. I prefer the term *treatment* because that word connotes thoroughness and careful preparation—what any writer should insist on bringing to each and every one of his or her projects.

You probably also know that the word *treatment* is used by screen-writers and refers to the delineation of a scene-by-scene outline so that it actually reads like a story, albeit a condensed one. (According to Stewart Bronfeld in his book, *Writing for Film and Television*, the term "treatment" originated in the early days of moviemaking when scouts would screen published books looking for material that could be given "the movie treatment"—in other words be successfully made into a movie.)

What is a Treatment?

In a treatment you lay out the contents of your proposed feature as concisely as you can—but not so concisely that it's merely a synopsis. The difference between a treatment and the draft of the essay itself is that the treatment does not include finishing touches like detailed explanations, analyses, elaborate descriptions, or fully rendered dramatic moments.

You may also be wondering about the connection between a treatment and an outline. Superficially, a treatment resembles a paragraph of conventional prose, whereas an outline, in case you haven't yet studied the preceding chapter, is a skeletal breakdown of headings that describe the contents of sections of the proposed feature. In terms of purpose, the distinction is simply this: Whereas the job of an outline is to remind the writer of key points to cover in the work (and specifically where in the work to cover them), the treatment gives the writer a sense of the essay in miniature, enough to see how everything hangs together coherently.

This chapter will guide you through the process of writing a treatment. If you follow this process closely, the actual drafting of the feature should proceed quickly and smoothly, and diminish the likelihood of false starts or conceptual blocks.

Writing the Treatment

The best way to write the treatment, provided you've completed a formal outline and haven't let too much time lapse, is to plunge right in. Doing a treatment should feel more like daybook writing than formal drafting. Unlike daybook writing, though, you try to stay focused on your topic and on the major points you want to get across by keeping your outline at your side. Also try to incorporate as many particular details as you can without spending time worrying about it. When it's time to write the first draft (which will occupy our attention in Chapters 7, 8, and 9), the goal will be thoroughness, but for now, the goal is to get the guts of the feature onto paper.

Two Kinds of Treatments

You can write a treatment as a continuous narrative or break it up into storyboard form. I suggest you experiment with both types to see which one works best for you.

The Narrative Treatment

To prepare a narrative treatment, start writing your feature as if you were relating your thoughts to a friend. Your chief concern is to transform an outline into continuous prose. You're not going to concern yourself yet with well-made sentences or precise words, only with story progression.

Here's an example of how one might begin the treatment for the stargazing feature we outlined in the previous chapter. Note how the writer includes bracketed reminders about how to elaborate on a particular point during the drafting stage.

> My next-door neighbor is a homemaker and a cosmologist. On most clear nights I see her out on her terrace squinting through her telescope [be sure to mention what kind]. Gradually I began to wonder what it was about the night sky that captivated her so. Oh sure, I like to feast my eyes on a full moon or wish upon a star now and then—but beyond that, what's to fascinate? Okay, maybe Saturn's rings, maybe Jupiter's four largest moons, maybe the fuzzy patterns on the surface of Mars—but am I being cynical when I assume that seeing them once would be enough? So when I decided I would talk to my neighbor about her stargazing, I decided that I would begin by voicing my skepticism.

As you can see, the writer is aiming to generate a sense of anticipation that only a narrative treatment can provide. Later, he'll be able to transfer that narrative progression to the draft itself.

The Storyboard Treatment

Storyboarding is another screenwriter's term, but it is commonly used in a wide range of professional-writing contexts. People in business and industry who write proposals, user manuals, feasibility studies, environmental-impact reports, and the like often use the storyboard approach for their treatment. Screenwriters (not just of feature films, but of documentaries and instructional videos as well) prepare storyboards by describing each and every visual moment of the planned film on index cards and then tacking these cards onto a corkboard in a tentative sequence. The nice thing about placing story bits on individual cards is that you can shuffle the cards around easily, or get rid of cards, or add new cards, in order to experiment with a variety of possible sequences. It makes organizing a creative work both fun and efficient.

To prepare a storyboard treatment of your lifewriting feature, lay in a supply of 4 x 6 index cards, ruled or unruled, white or some other color or a combination of colors if you think you might enjoy "color coding" the sections of your piece. You will also need as many pushpins as cards. And, unless you don't mind nailing cards to your walls, you will need a corkboard large enough to accommodate as many as a hundred or more index cards.

In case you're curious, I myself happen to be a storyboard fan. There's a satisfying visual dimension to storyboarding that even a computer screen can't match. I experience an element of play, too. Don't ask me why, but I feel like a kid surrounded by toys when surrounded by index cards that I can shuffle around, revise, tear up, and link together (with paper clips, strips of tape, whatever). Check out the sidebar on the next page to see how I first storyboarded Chapter 1.

Using a Treatment Productively

When I'm working on a book or article of any kind, I move as quickly as possible from outline to storyboard treatment to retain momentum. So, if you've finished your treatment, congratulations are in order—but no resting on your laurels yet. You have the draft left to write and then revise. If you take too long a break at this juncture, you'll lose steam—not a good idea; it's often tough getting that writing engine revved up once it cools.

A Few of My Storyboard Cards for Chapter 1

Card 1—Anatomy of Lifewriting

Words like "biography" and "autobiography" are too formalistic; other terms like "personal essays" or "creative nonfiction" don't convey the purpose of such writing, which is to entertain and edify readers with <u>your</u> experiences, or the experiences of others.

"Lifewriting" is good ol' Anglo-Saxon, emphasizing the act of writing about *your* <u>life</u> (or the lives of others), not just about an abstract concept.

Card 2—Formal Definition of Lifewriting

A lively, dramatic, sometimes humorous, usually short (500–4000 words) or book-length prose work about a person or persons or about a person-centered topic.

Card 3—My Own Experiences with School Themes (Yech!)

They tended to stifle my creativity, not stimulate it. <u>Some teachers actually used writing as a form of punishment! But for me, writing was always a labor of love, so I was not deterred.</u>

Card 4—Cultivating Basic Writing Habits—1

Take time to write every day. The most important part of learning to write is to write—regularly, habitually, without excuses. The easiest excuse would-be writers make: "I'm so busy that I don't have time to write."

Card 5—Cultivating Basic Writing Habits—2A

Write with good reader-based as well as writer-based motives in mind. People write to impress, to make money, to get rich and famous, to get even. These are the sorts of writer-based motives that should be secondary at best; better writer-based motives might include the desire to champion an unsung hero in your family or publicize your best achievements as a carpenter or lawyer or tennis player.

So, give yourself a *tiny* break. As you relax a bit with your favorite beverage (Sorry, nonalcoholic only; we'll uncork the Champagne at the end of Chapter 10.), place the following two printouts in front of you:

- Your formal outline
- Your treatment

The outline lets you see how you've organized your ideas; the treatment provides a feeling for the continuity of ideas. The latter should seem to grow harmoniously out of the former.

EXERCISES

1. Practice storyboarding first by preparing a scratch outline of a recent travel experience, then turn each segment of the outline into a storyboard card. Use as many cards as you think necessary to establish a sequence of events and impressions that comprise this trip.

2. Prepare a narrative or storyboard treatment of a character profile. Begin by interviewing the individual; next, use the printout of the interview to form an outline; finally, develop the outline into a treatment.

3. Write a treatment for a feature in which you write about your workplace. Make it a people-centered feature that includes profiles of administrators, middle-management personnel, and technical or support staff.

Part Two

Ready, Get Set, Start Drafting!

Drafting I:
Wielding Opening Magic

In this Chapter
~ Get your feature off to a flying start
~ Types of effective openings

After about a week's worth of daybook scribbling, researching, outlining, and treatment writing, you will be set to write your first draft. Like the treatment, the first draft affords you plenty of room to try new things on the spur of the moment. The emphasis, however, shifts from stirring in the basic ingredients to cooking the finished meal.

A first draft consists of three stages:

1. Wielding opening magic (getting your feature off to a flying start);

2. Putting meat on the bones (developing the key points);

3. Wrapping things up in a satisfying manner (writing the conclusion).

This and the next two chapters will guide you through the drafting process, one stage at a time. The six chapters comprising Part III will guide you through the revision stages.

All set to begin drafting your lifewriting feature? Let's get to work.

Get Your Feature Off to a Flying Start

One of the most important principles of writing, which I find myself stressing repeatedly in my classes, is audience awareness. Being audience-aware does not mean pandering to or trying to "psych out" the likes and dislikes of your readers; that rather contradicts the very purpose of writing, which is to bring something new and unanticipated to your readers' experience. On the other hand, it does mean being sensitive to basic expectations. Along with being clear and entertaining, this means following through on the information promised by your title and made explicit in your introduction.

Here's a little game you can play that works for me when I'm at my computer, goaded by a blank screen and that infernal blinking cursor: Think of your readers as busy people who nevertheless are eager to be swept up by a fascinating piece of writing, and so are quite willing to grant you a few minutes of their time to engage them. If your piece appears in a magazine they're browsing through, the title is probably the first thing they'll consider—which is why it's important to come up with strong titles (see Chapter 5). But the acid test, as the cliché goes, will be your opening.

Without being gimmicky about it, your opening (which can be any number of paragraphs depending on length and approach, but is usually one or two) should convey three things to your readers—not necessarily in this order:

- Introduce, or at least hint at, the topic of the piece
- Generate curiosity about the subject
- Project a lively or amusing or energetic tone of voice

Read the following opening paragraph of a personal essay by Joseph Epstein; then, before continuing, try to determine for yourself whether the author succeeded in conveying the three ingredients listed above.

On the campus where I teach, there is a landmark, a large rock on which fraternity and sorority members paint their Greek letters, the political-minded their usually unobscene graffiti. The other day walking past it, I noticed that some less-than-advanced student of Latin had written "Veni, vidi, vici." Instantly, my mind rejoined, "Veni, vidi, vici / Your mother looks like Nietzsche." Why does my mind do this? Where do such items come from? What sort of thing is this for a man in his fifties to be thinking?

Ought I seek, as they say, professional help?

Joseph Epstein, "Toys in My Attic," from *With My Trousers Rolled: Familiar Essays*. Norton, 1995.

As you may have guessed, Epstein's essay is about mind-play, the childlike inclinations, especially of those who love language, to romp through the playroom of words and come up with weird combinations and associations. You also probably noticed that Epstein's title, "Toys in My Attic," is itself an example of the mind-play he writes about.

Three Common Mistakes Writers Make with Openings

• The "Biblical" or "*David Copperfield*" opening. So named because the writer erroneously assumes one has to begin at the absolute beginning of things. A short essay about childhood fantasies should not begin with the creation of the universe or with the circumstances surrounding your birth, as Dickens describes his main character's birth in that 800-page novel.

• The Global opening. In this kind of opening, the writer feels compelled to place the topic at hand in the largest possible context. In a short feature about growing up on a dairy farm, one writer opened with an overview of dairy farming in the United States!

• The Gimmicky opening. If anything is worse than not caring about piquing your reader's curiosity at the outset, it is trying to do so with trickery.

Types of Effective Openings

Epstein begins by recounting a specific incident, walking past a large rock covered with fraternity and sorority graffiti. This is known as an *anecdotal* opening. The intent is to engage the reader with a little story. Generally speaking, stories capture the attention of readers more rapidly than explanations or descriptions.

Another effective opening type is the "I-Am-Here" (or "You-Are-Here") opening—to provide quick, dramatic situational or geographical orientation. Here is how the poet-naturalist-essayist Diane Ackerman opens her book about her experience learning to fly a plane:

> You are seated tensely in the cockpit of a single-engine plane, one hand crushing the control wheel as if it were a test of grip strength at a fair, the other half-opening the throttle with a tentativeness that has nonetheless sent you charging down the runway at 40 mph, toward the thick, wreck-hungry forest edging the airport, called Sapsucker Woods. Half the runway is spent behind you, the air is a single loud growl of straining engine, the end of the runway is lunging up at you like a punch, and at your right, an instructor is screaming, *It's now or never!* ....
>
> Diane Ackerman, *On Extended Wings*. New York: Atheneum, 1985.

Ackerman is quite aware that if she wants her readers to stay with her for more than a few pages she must demonstrate right off the bat (or airplane throttle, in this case) that a book about learning to fly will make for exciting reading.

Before reading on, see if you can pick out the techniques she employs.

Most obvious is her use of the second person (sometimes referred to as the "you" approach), instead of the first or third person. This technique creates a keen sense of You-Are-There. One gets the impression of being inside the cockpit, feeling the excitement and tension of the moment.

Another technique is vivid imagery, achieved by way of strong verbs and figurative language—similes, metaphors, personification, and

such—a hallmark of Ackerman's style; she is, not surprisingly, a distinguished poet:

- … one hand *crushing* the control wheel *as if it were a test of grip* strength at a fair
- … the air is a single *loud growl* of straining engine
- … the end of the runway is *lunging* up at you *like a punch*

Similar to the I-Am-Here opening is the "Stage Setting" opening, where
the essayist wishes to orient the reader as concisely and as vividly as
possible to the setting and situation. It doesn't convey the same degree
of dramatic immediacy as I-Am-Here (the subject matter may make that
inappropriate), but it can be just as captivating, as George Orwell's opening paragraph to his famous essay, "A Hanging," demonstrates:

> It was in Burma, a sodden morning of the rains. A
> sickly light, like yellow tinfoil, was slanting over the high
> walls into the jail yard. We were waiting outside the con-
> demned cells, a row of sheds fronted with double bars,
> like small animal cages. Each cell measured about ten
> feet by ten and was quite bare within except for a plank
> bed and a pot for drinking water. In some of them, brown
> silent men were squatting at the inner bars, with their
> blankets draped round them. These were the condemned
> men, due to be hanged within the next week or two.
>
> "A Hanging," from *Shooting an Elephant and Other Essays*. New York:
> Harcourt, 1950.

Notice what Orwell is able to accomplish with a mere six precisely-
crafted sentences:

(1) the geographical setting: Burma, during monsoon season;
(2) the immediate setting: a jail yard;
(3) the situation: condemned prisoners are soon to die;
(4) the grim ambiance: tiny cage-like cells with planks for beds;

a sense of hopelessness reinforced by the sickly yellow light, the huddled and silent prisoners;

(5) a curiosity-stimulating tidbit: Why are the narrator and his associates there? What are they waiting for?

Let's consider another opening strategy, what we might call the "What-Is-Going-On-Here?" or the "puzzle" opening: a curious situation that the author gradually elucidates. Here is how Daphne Merkin begins her essay, "Trouble in the Tribe":

> I've been trying to lose my religion for years, now, but it refuses to go away. Just when I think I've shaken it—put it firmly behind me, a piece of my obscurantist past no longer suited to the faithless life I now lead—it turns up again, dogging me. You'd think it would be easy, particularly in a city like New York, where no one cares whether or not you believe in God; even my friends who do would be hard put to explain why, other than by alluding knowingly to Pascal's wager, in which the odds favor the believer. But as the world becomes a more bewildering place almost by the week, I find myself longing for what I thought I'd never long for again: a sense of community in the midst of the impersonal vastness, a tribe to call my own.
>
> Daphne Merkin, "Trouble in the Tribe," from *The Best American Essays*, 2001 edition. Kathleen Norris (ed.). Boston: Houghton Mifflin, 2001.

In this opening, Merkin not only introduces the theme of the essay—her own struggle to find personal value in adhering to traditional religious views and practices in modern American secular and heterogeneous culture, but she is able to convey a sense of that struggle through her manner of expression ("Just when I feel I've shaken it ..."). The rest of the essay is, in one sense, an elaboration of that struggle. One moment we find her drawn to the beauty and mystery of orthodox Judaism; another moment we find her unable to resist acts of sacrilege, like eating non-Kosher food on a religious holiday. She also sets her personal predicament against those of more public figures like Senator Joseph Lieberman, the first Jew to become a candidate for vice president of the United States.

A fourth type of opening is what we might call the "Nugget-of-Wisdom" opening, an opening flash of insight that delights as much as it informs.

Here is how Edward Hoagland begins his essay about our collective experience of water, titled "Earth's Eye":

> Water is our birthplace. We need and love it. In a bathtub, or by a lake or at the sea, we go to it for rest, refreshment, and solace. "I'm going to the water," people say when August comes and they crave a break. The sea is a democracy, so big it's free of access, often a bus or subway ride away, a meritocracy, sink or swim, and yet a swallower of grief because of its boundless scale—beyond the horizon, the home of icebergs, islands, whales. Tears alone are a mysterious, magisterial solvent that bring a smile, a softening of hard thoughts, lend us a merciful and inexpensive respite, almost like half an hour at the beach. In any landscape, in fact, a pond or creek catches and centers our attention as magnetically as if it were, in Thoreau's phrase, "earth's eye."
>
> Edward Hoagland, "Earth's Eye," from *The Best American Essays*, 2000, edition. Alan Lightman (ed.). Boston: Houghton Mifflin.

Hoagland's four-word opening sentence, "Water is our birthplace," kindles both our intellect and our imagination at once, reminding us not only that all life originated in the sea, but that we all harbor an intimate connection to water as if it were our primal mother. If Hoagland had instead written, "Water is where all life originated," the impact would not have been nearly as great.

And then there's what we might call the "startling-disclosure" opening—a word or phrase or allusion that doesn't seem to fit the context, and so secures our curiosity immediately. The award-winning novelist

Jonathan Franzen uses this kind of opening for his essay on how Alzheimer's Disease affected his father:

> Here's a memory: On an overcast morning in February, 1996, I received in the mail from my mother, in St. Louis, a Valentine's package containing one pinkly romantic greeting card, two four-ounce Mr. Goodbars, one hollow red filigree heart on a loop of thread, and one copy of a neuropathologist's report on my father's brain autopsy.
>
> Jonathan Franzen, "My Father's Brain: What Alzheimer's Takes Away," from *The Best American Magazine Writing*, 2002, edition. Sebastian Junger (ed.). New York: HarperCollins, 2002.

A neuropathologist's report on a brain autopsy in the same sentence as a pinkly romantic greeting card? Startling, all right—but Franzen is not using any mere sit-up-and-pay-attention-to-me gimmick. The juxtaposition with emblems of love and a grim emblem of mortality is precisely the effect Franzen wishes to create in an essay that is ultimately a moving eulogy to his father.

EXERCISE

Study the following openings to lifewriting essays. In each case identify (a) the opening technique the author uses; and (b) the subject of the essay, based on clues the opening provides; and (c) what the author does (if anything) to make you want to keep reading:

> I had been lying on my back, taking notes, looking up into the crystals and into that blue that still amazes me—blue so blue it was as if my eyes had broken; blue so blue that it was like gas that faded away into more and more intense blue violet; beauty so expansive I could not contain it—I had to break to let it in. The first time I had been in an Antarctic ice cave, months earlier, the person who took me there said that often people who go down into crevasses and into ice caves are so overcome

by the blue that it makes them cry. I remembered that as I lay there on my back, taking notes, trying to draw the crystals that hung like blooms of flowers above me, trying to figure out where the blue began and where it ended.

Gretchen Legher, "Moments of Being: An Antarctic Quintet," *The Georgia Review* 56, Winter 2002.

As soon as the 2003 World Taxidermy Championships opened, the heads came rolling in the door. There were foxes and moose and freeze-dried wild turkeys; mallards and buffalo and chipmunks and wolves; weasels and buffleheads and bobcats and jackdaws; big fish and little fish and razor-backed boar. The deer came in herds, in carloads, and on pallets: dozens and dozens of whitetail and roe; half-deer and whole deer and deer with deformities, sneezing and glowering and nuzzling and yawning; does chewing apples and bucks nibbling leaves. There were millions of eyes, boxes and bowls of them; some as small as a lentil and some as big as a poached egg.

Susan Orlean, "Lifelike," *The New Yorker*, June 9, 2003.

In January of this year [2003] British newspapers began running articles about Robert Smith, a surgeon at Falkirk and District Royal Infirmary, in Scotland. Smith had amputated the legs of two patients at their request, and he was planning on carrying out a third amputation when the trust that runs his hospital stopped him. These patients were not physically sick. Their legs did not need to be amputated for any medical reason, Nor were they incompetent, according to the psychiatrists who examined them. They simply wanted to have their legs cut off.

Carl Elliott, "A New Way To Be Mad," *The Atlantic Monthly*, December 2000.

8

Drafting II: Bodybuilding

In this Chapter
~ Principal methods of bodybuilding
~ Statistics
~ Comparison
~ Classification and division
~ Example, case-in-point
~ Quotation
~ Characterization, dialogue

What the opening of an essay promises, the body of the essay must deliver. This is known as "developing your ideas," but I like to use a *bodybuilding* metaphor because it implies adding not just bulk to a framework, but musculature. In other words, good essay development *strengthens*, not merely fills out, the essay. Now that you've worked hard on writing a strong opening, one that has introduced your topic in a lively manner, now that you've persuaded busy people to set aside a chunk of their time to read what you have to say, you must deliver the goods.

Principal Methods of Bodybuilding

What is the best way to reinforce the main idea of your essay? You can do some by making good use of any combination of the following six methods of development:

- Statistics
- Comparison
- Classification and division
- Example, case-in-point
- Quotation
- Characterization, dialogue

By using these bodybuilding elements, you are telling your readers, "I don't expect you to take my word for these claims; I want you see for yourself!" Of course, the examples you provide must be authentic and not exaggerated or distorted. Readers implicitly trust writers of nonfiction to diligently adhere to this norm. Let's say you are working on a feature about the way pets contribute significantly to the psychological well-being of elderly residents in a nursing home. Readers will not only expect you to provide cases-in-point, such as detailed profiles of those men and women in nursing homes whose physical and psychological health improved demonstrably after being given a pet cat or dog to care for, but they will also assume that the individuals you describe are real, not fabricated. Oh, sure, you can use *hypothetical* situations as examples (they're not nearly as convincing as actual examples), but you must make it clear to your readers that is what they are.

Let's take a close look at each of these methods.

Statistics

"Stats," as they're affectionately called—hard data—do not crop up often in lifewriting; but used judiciously, they can add conviction to particular assertions. Notice how colorfully Mark Twain uses statistics in this passage from *Life on the Mississippi*, the chronicle of his experiences as a riverboat pilot. At one point he describes the nature of "cutoffs" or "necks" in the river—horseshoe-shaped bends that the powerful current eventually cuts through:

> Once there was a neck opposite Port Hudson, Louisiana, which was only half a mile across, in its narrowest place. You could walk across there in fifteen minutes; but if you made the journey around the cape on a raft, you traveled thirty-five miles to accomplish the same thing. In 1722 the river darted through that neck, deserted its old bed, and thus shortened itself thirty-five miles. In the same way it shortened itself twenty-five miles at Black Hawk Point in 1699.... Since my own day on the Mississippi, cutoffs have been made at Hurricane Island; at Island 100; at Napoleon, Arkansas; at Walnut Bend; and at Council Bend.

And then, as if worried that so much statistical data might bore his readers, Twain lapses into his famous satirical wit:

> Now, if I wanted to be one of those ponderous scientific people, and "let on" to prove what had occurred in the remote past by what had occurred in a given time in the recent past ... what an opportunity is here! ... In the space of one hundred and seventy-six years the Lower Mississippi had shortened itself two hundred and forty-two miles. That is an average of a trifle over one mile and a third per year. Therefore, any calm person, who is not blind or idiotic, can see that in the Old Oölithic Silurian Period, just a million years ago next November, the Lower Mississippi River was upwards of one million three hundred thousand miles long, and stuck out over the Gulf of Mexico like a fishing rod.
>
> Mark Twain, *Life on the Mississippi* (1883). *Mississippi Writings*. New York: Library of America, 1982.

The statistical data Twain uses—the Mississippi shortening itself by 25 miles in 1699, by 35 miles in 1722; names of the locations at which the cutoffs had been created; the total number of miles by which the river had shortened itself over the past 170 years, and so on—all contribute to his satiric purpose, which is to contrast the "down home" reference to the cutoffs at the beginning of the excerpt with the "ponderous" scientific ones that immediately follow.

Comparison

Comparison is an effective way to help your readers see things in larger contexts. "The winters in Anchorage are mild," someone tells you. "Compared to what?" you ask. "Well, they're mild compared to those in Fairbanks, but compared to the winters in San Diego, I suppose you could say they're pretty cold."

Sometimes comparisons are made because the similarities and differences between two people, or two cultures, or two of anything, are intrinsically interesting. The Civil War historian Bruce Catton painted a memorable, often anthologized comparison between generals Ulysses S. Grant and Robert E. Lee during the surrender at Appomattox Courthouse in Virginia in 1865:

> When Ulysses S. Grant and Robert E. Lee met in the parlor of a modest house at Appomattox Court House, Virginia, on April 9, 1865, to work out the terms for the surrender of Lee's Army of Northern Virginia, a great chapter in American life came to a close, and a great new chapter began.
>
> These men were bringing the Civil War to its virtual finish. To be sure, other armies had yet to surrender, and for a few days the fugitive Confederate government would struggle desperately and vainly, trying to find some way to go on living now that its chief support was gone. But in effect it was all over when Grant and Lee signed the papers. And the little room where they wrote out the terms was the scene of one of the poignant, dramatic contrasts in American history.

They were two strong men, these oddly different generals, and they represented the strengths of two conflicting currents that, through them, had come into final collision.

Back of Robert E. Lee was the notion that the old aristocratic concept might somehow survive and be dominant in American life.

Lee was tidewater Virginia, and in his background were family, culture, and tradition... the age of chivalry transplanted to a New World which was making its own legends and its own myths. He embodied a way of life that had come down through the age of knighthood and the English country squire. America was a land that was beginning all over again, dedicated to nothing much more complicated than the rather hazy belief that all men had equal rights and should have an equal chance in the world. In such a land Lee stood for the feeling that it was somehow of advantage to human society to have a pronounced inequality in the social structure. There should be a leisure class, backed by ownership of land; in turn, society itself should be keyed to the land as the chief source of wealth and influence. It would bring forth (according to this ideal) a class of men with a strong sense of obligation to the community; men who lived not to gain advantage for themselves, but to meet the solemn obligations which had been laid on them by the very fact that they were privileged. From them the country would get its leadership; to them it could look for the higher values—of thought, of conduct, of personal deportment—to give it strength and virtue.

Lee embodied the noblest elements of this aristocratic idea. Through him, the landed nobility justified itself. For four years, the Southern states had fought a desperate war to uphold the ideals for which Lee stood. In the end, it almost seemed as if the Confederacy fought for Lee; as if he himself was the Confederacy ... the best thing that the way of life for which the Confederacy stood could ever have to offer. He had passed into legend before Appomattox. Thousands of tired, underfed, poorly clothed Confederate soldiers, long since past the simple enthusiasm of the early days of the struggle, somehow considered Lee the symbol of everything for which they had been willing to die. But they could not quite put this feeling into words. If the Lost Cause, sanctified by so much heroism and so many deaths, had a living justification, its justification was General Lee.

Grant, the son of a tanner on the Western frontier, was everything Lee was not. He had come up the hard way and embodied nothing in particular except the eternal toughness and sinewy fiber of the men who grew up beyond the mountains. He was one of a body of men who owed reverence and obeisance to no one, who were self-reliant to a fault, who cared hardly anything for the past but who had a sharp eye for the future.

These frontier men were the precise opposites of the tidewater aristocrats. Back of them, in the great surge that had taken people over the Alleghenies and into the opening Western country, there was a deep, implicit dissatisfaction with a past that had settled into grooves. They stood for democracy, not from any reasoned conclusion about the proper ordering of human society, but simply because they had grown up in the middle of democracy and knew how it worked. Their society might have privileges, but they would be privileges each man had won for himself. Forms and patterns meant nothing. No man was born to anything except perhaps to a chance to show how far he could rise. Life was competition.

Yet along with this feeling had come a deep sense of belonging to a national community. The Westerner, who developed a farm, opened shop, or set up in business as a trader, could hope to prosper only as his own community prospered—and his community ran from the Atlantic to the Pacific and from Canada down to Mexico. If the land was settled, with towns and highways and accessible markets, he could better himself. He saw his fate in terms of the nation's own destiny. As its horizons expanded so did his. He had, in other words, an acute dollars-and-cents stake in the continued growth and development of his country.

And that, perhaps, is where the contrast between Grant and Lee becomes most striking. The Virginia aristocrat, inevitably, saw himself in relation to his own region. He lived in a static society which could endure almost anything except change. Instinctively, his first loyalty would go to the locality in which that society existed. He would fight to the limit of endurance to defend it, because in defending it he was defending everything that gave his own life its deepest meaning.

The Westerner, on the other hand, would fight with an equal tenacity for the broader concept of society. He fought so because everything he lived by was tied to growth, expansion, and a constantly widening horizon. What he lived by would survive or fall with the nation itself. He could not possibly stand by unmoved in the face of an attempt to destroy the Union. He would combat it with everything he had, because he could only see it as an effort to cut the ground out from under his feet.

So Grant and Lee were in complete contrast, representing two diametrically opposed elements in American life. Grant was the modern man emerging; beyond him, ready to come on the stage, was the great age of steel and machinery, of crowded cities and a restless burgeoning vitality. Lee might have ridden down from the old age of chivalry, lance in hand, silken banner fluttering over his head. Each man was the perfect champion of his cause, drawing both his strengths and his weaknesses from the people he led.

Yet it was not all contrast, after all. Different as they were—in background, in personality, in underlying aspiration—these two great soldiers had much in common. Under everything else, they were marvelous fighters. Furthermore, their fighting qualities were really very much alike.

Each man had, to begin with, the great virtue of utter tenacity and fidelity. Grant fought his way down the Mississippi Valley in spite of acute personal discouragement and profound military handicaps. Lee hung on in the trenches at Petersburg after hope itself had died. In each man there was an indomitable quality ... the born fighter's refusal to give up as long as he can still remain on his feet and lift his two fists.

Daring and resourcefulness they had, too; the ability to think faster and move faster than the enemy. These were the qualities which gave Lee the dazzling campaigns of Second Manassas and Chancellorsville and won Vicksburg for Grant.

Lastly, and perhaps greatest of all, there was the ability, at the end, to turn quickly from war to peace once the fighting was over. Out of the way these two men behaved at Appomattox came the possibility of a peace of reconciliation. It was a possibility not wholly realized, in the years to come, but which did, in the end, help the two sections to become one nation again ... after a war whose bitterness might have seemed to make such a reunion wholly impossible. No part of either man's life became him more than the part he played in their brief meeting in the McLean house at Appomattox. Their behavior there put all succeeding generations of Americans in their debt. Two great Americans, Grant and Lee—very different, yet under everything very much alike. Their encounter at

Appomattox was one of the great moments of American history.

> Bruce Catton, "Grant and Lee: A Study in Contrasts," *The American Story*, edited by Earl Schenk Miers. Copyright 1956, 1984 by the United States Historical Society.

Did you notice Catton's manner of comparison? The first two paragraphs introduce the background. After an opening sentence that quickly establishes the focus of the essay, Catton describes the context: "These two men were bringing the Civil War to its virtual finish." The third paragraph segues from background to an introductory look at Grant and Lee: "They were two strong men".... but represented conflicting strengths. The next two paragraphs are devoted to Lee alone; the two paragraphs after that to Grant alone; finally they are compared together—first in terms of their contrasting features, then in terms of their similarities.

Classification and Division

This organizing principle is common with procedural or explanatory features, but it can come in handy for lifewriting on occasion. If you're writing about personality types, you probably would find these schemata useful.

Here is how you might structure such an essay using the classification schema:

- Fast Lane (Type A) personalities
- Middle Lane (Type B) personalities
- Slow Lane (Type C) personalities
- Off the Road personalities (and you might contrast this extreme at the other end of the scale with "Jet Stream personalities"—those ultra-aggressive types for whom even the fast lane is too slow. Nothing slower than a Lear Jet will do for those types.)

Division schemata are similar to classification ones, but instead of categorizing wholes (Fast Lane types, Slow Lane types), you're breaking a whole into parts. If you were writing a profile of someone from a Freudian psychoanalytic perspective, for example, you might adopt Freud's division schema for the mind to describe the dynamics of that individual's personality:

- The *id*: the primal mind from which instinctive desires and energies emanate
- The *ego*: that aspect of mind which seeks a self-satisfying middle ground between the pleasure-drive (libido) and social regulation
- The *superego*: that aspect of mind which abides by laws, morals, ethical principles

In the following short essay, "Of Gardens," Francis Bacon (1561–1626), the English philosopher, statesman, and contemporary of Shakespeare, expresses his delight in classifying certain types of garden flowers for certain times of the year, and for their particular smells:

God Almighty first planted a garden. And indeed it is the purest of human pleasures. It is the greatest refreshment to the spirits of man, without which buildings and palaces are but gross handy-works: and a man shall ever see that when ages grow to civility and elegancy, men come to build stately sooner than to garden finely, as if gardening were the greater perfection. I do hold it, in the royal ordering of gardens, there ought to be gardens for all the months in the year, in which severally things of beauty may be then in season. For December and January and the latter part of November, you must take such things as are green all winter: holly, ivy, bays, juniper, cypress-trees, yew, pineapple-trees; and myrtles, if they be stoved [kept in hothouses]; and sweet marjoram, warm-set [kept in a warm and sunny location]. There followeth, for the latter part of January and February, the mezereontree, which then blossoms; crocus vernus, both the yellow and the grey; primroses, anemones, the early tulippa, hyacinthus orientalis, chamiris [dwarf iris], fritillaria. For March, there come violets, specially the single blue, which are the earliest; the yellow daffodil, the daisy, the almond-tree in blossom, the peach-tree in blossom, the corne-lian-tree in blossom, sweet-briar. In April follow the double white violet, the wall-flower, the stock-gillyflower, the cowslip, flower-de-luces, and lilies of all natures; rosemary flowers, the toulippa, the double peony, the pale daffo-dil, the French honeysuckle; the cherry-tree in blossom, the damson and plum-trees in blossom, the white-thorn in leaf, the lilac-tree. In May and June come pinks of all sorts, specially the blush pink; roses of all kinds, except the musk, which comes later; honeysuckles, strawberries, bugloss, columbine; the French marigold, flos Africanus; cherry-tree in fruit, ribes [currants], figs in fruit, rasps [rasp-berries], vine-flowers, lavender in flowers; the sweet satyrian, with the white flower; herba muscaria, lilium convallium, the apple-tree in blossom. In July come gilly-flowers of all varieties, musk-roses, the lime-tree in blos-som, early pears and plums in fruit, jennertings, coldins [lily of the valley]. In August come plums of all sorts in fruit, pears, apricots, barberries, filberts, musk-melons, monk-hoods of all colours. In September come grapes, apples, poppies of all colours, peaches, melocotones [very large peaches], nectarines, cornelians, wardens [a variety of pear], quinces. In October and the beginning of November come services, medlars, bullaces, roses cut or removed [i.e., transplanted] to come late, hollyhocks, and such like. These particulars are for the climate of London; but my meaning is perceived, that you may have *ver pepetuum* [perpetual spring], as the place affords.

And because the breath of flowers is far sweeter in the air (where it comes and goes like the warbling of music) than in the hand, therefore nothing is more fit for that delight than to know what be the flowers and plants that do best perfume the air. Roses, damask and red, are fast flowers of their smells [i.e., that retain their smells], so that you may walk by a whole row of them, and find nothing of their sweetness, yea, though it be in a morning's dew. Bays likewise yield no smell as they grow, rosemary little, nor sweet marjoram. That which above all others yields the sweetest smell in the air is the violet, specially the white double violet, which comes twice a year, about the middle of April and about Bartholomew-tide [St. Bartholomew's day, August 24]. Next to that is the musk-rose. Then the strawberry-leaves dying, with a most excellent cordial smell. Then the flower of the vines; it is a little dust, like the dust of a bent, which grows upon the cluster in the first coming forth. Then sweet-briar. Then wall-flowers, which are very delightful to set under a parlour or lower chamber window. Then pinks and gilly-flowers, specially the matted pink and clove gillyflower. Then the flowers of the lime-tree. Then the honeysuck-les, so they be somewhat afar off. Of bean-flowers I speak not, because they are field flowers. But those which perfume the air most delightfully, not passed by as the rest, but being trodden upon and crushed, are three: that is, burnet, wild thyme, and water-mints. Therefore you are to set whole alleys [foot-paths] of them, to have the pleasure when you walk or tread.

Francis Bacon, "Of Gardens" (1597).

What I find so intriguing about this essay (along with the early-modern English syntax and the exotic flower names) is the way that Bacon satisfies his scientific impulse for taxonomy and precise nomenclature while at the same time celebrating the almost overwhelming sensory effusions of gardens.

Example, Case-in-Point

Examples or cases-in-point make your assertions convincing and understandable. If you claim that nursing home residents given pet cats or dogs become content, readers will expect you (a) to give examples and (b) that the examples will answer their question, "What do you mean by 'content'?" By the way, the difference between an example and a case-in-point is simply that the latter is a more elaborate kind of example. If you were to create a detailed profile for one of the nursing-home residents in order to monitor her day-to-day changes in personality and temperament, then you would be using a case-in-point, not merely an example.

In his famous biography of the great English lexicographer, poet, and critic Samuel Johnson, James Boswell early on calls attention to Johnson's "morbid melancholy," that had been afflicting him since he was twenty. "For example?" the readers ask, their curiosity aroused. Boswell is quite accommodating:

> [For example], while he was at Lichfield, in the college vacation of the year 1729, he felt himself overwhelmed with an horrible hypochondria, with perpetual irritation, fretfulness, and impatience; and with a dejection, gloom, and despair which made existence misery .... Johnson, upon the first violent attack of this disorder, strove to overcome it by forcible exertions. He frequently walked to Birmingham and back again, and tried many other expedients, but all in vain.
>
> James Boswell, *Life of Johnson* (1791). Oxford University Press, 1980.

Quotation

Unlike journalists or scholars who quote people for their authoritative comments, lifewriters quote people to add color and depth to their character (dialogue—conversation between two or more persons—see below—also serves this purpose), and to capture a key motif in the essay. Notice how Loren Eiseley uses this technique in this excerpt from an essay on Captain James Cook's voyage to Antarctica:

> In 1773 Cook first crossed the Antarctic Circle, where, in the words of one of his scientist passengers, "We were …wrapped in thick fogs, beaten with showers of rain, sleet, hail and snow …and daily ran the risk of being shipwrecked." Cook himself, after four separate and widely removed plunges across the Circle, speaks, as does Homer, of lands "never to yield to the warmth of the sun." His description of an "inexpressibly horrid Antarctica" resounds like an Odyssean line. Incognita Australis had been circumnavigated at last, its population reduced to penguins.
>
> Loren Eiseley, *The Unexpected Universe*. New York: Harcourt, 1969.

What I find remarkable about this passage—indeed, of so much of Loren Eiseley's essays—is the skillful way in which he intertwines ancient, enchanting tales of exploration—like the mythic journey of Odysseus (from which the word "odyssey" is derived) as a motif for more modern voyages of discovery. In so doing, Eiseley demonstrates how exploration and the quest for knowledge are primal forces of human nature.

Characterization, Dialogue

Describing people, including revealing aspects of their temperament through dialogue, adds drama and richness to your lifewriting features. Try not to overuse dialogue, though. Brief but pithy quotation can go a long way, as the following passage from an autobiographical essay by Nancy Mairs, who once voluntarily committed herself to a mental institution because of debilitating depression, demonstrates:

> I was admitted to the hospital at night. I don't know why. It was a poor arrangement because it gave the whole transaction the flavor of an emergency, and I was quite panic-stricken enough without any extra theatrical effects. By this time I was sobbing reflexively, inconsolably, without cease. The admitting psychiatrist was a small Indian man (almost all the doctors there were foreigners working their way into the American system; if they were any

good they quickly moved on to better hospitals or private practice). Dr. Haque. His accent was so strong that I couldn't understand most of what he said. "Why are you here? Why are you here?" he asked. I kept shaking my head and choking on tears. The silliness of this scene, both of us strangled, one on the English language, and the other on grief, escaped me for several years. Before long, Dr. Haque abandoned attempts at communication, wrote several prescriptions, and sent me upstairs.

Nancy Mairs, "On Living behind Bars," from *Plaintext*. Tucson: University of Arizona Press, 1986.

Mairs uses only one line of dialogue, but note how effectively it completes the description of Dr. Haque. Of course, you can use dialogue as interactive conversation, as in the following encounter with Florida orange pickers that John McPhee recreates in his book-length essay about oranges and the orange-growing industry:

It was five minutes past three, and he [Doyle Waid] had picked twenty thousand oranges that day. He would get twenty-five dollars, and he seemed to be feeling pretty good about it. Picking a hundred boxes a day is impossible for most people, but for him it had become a minimum standard. After all, he was good at it, and he was in his prime as a picker. At the time, he was twenty-nine years old.

"I have made as high as forty-one dollars in a day," Waid told me.

"When did you do that?"

"Back in tangerines."

Each tangerine has to be removed from the tree with a pair of clippers or a plug will pull out of the skin. Tangerines pay three times as much as oranges, which are snapped from the tree with a fast turn of the wrist that is similar to the motion used by a baseball pitcher throwing a curve.

John McPhee, *Oranges*. New York: Farrar, Straus and Giroux, 1967.

McPhee is one of the best essayists in the business because of the way he is able to capture professionals involved in their work—no matter what kind of work; he has written about schoolmasters, geologists, civil engineers, athletes, environmentalists, mechanics, etc. with depth and realism.

EXERCISE

See if you can identify the bodybuilding elements in the following passages:

Great Skellig, that black rock with the lighthouse that blinks nightly at the black sea, is called Skellig Michael, for the Archangel, like those two other famous sea rocks on the coasts of Europe that are dedicated to the Saint. There the resemblance ends. Mount St. Michael in Cornwell and Mont Saint-Michel in Brittany are connected to the mainland by causeways. They are home to substantial communities of permanent residents and are easily accessible to tourists. Ireland's Skellig Michael lies at the end of a sea voyage. Except for the keepers of the light, the island is uninhabited. It is a place of sheer precipices and terrifying landings.

—Chet Raymo, *Honey from Stone: A Naturalist's Search for God*. New York: Penguin Books, 1987.

Anne [Boleyn's] civic reception and the route she followed were much the same as Katherine of Aragon's welcome to London thirty-two years earlier, and the pageants—staged at great cost to citizens—were on similar themes. As was customary, free wine ran in the conduits for the crowds lining the streets, children made speeches, and choirs raised their voices in honour of the new Queen. The verses recited in one pageant were composed by Nicholas Udall, Provost of Eton College from 1534 to 1541, and ended in the chorus: "Honour and grace be to our Queen Anne!"

Alison Weir, *The Six Wives of Henry VIII*. NY: Grove, 1991.

9

Drafting III: Calling It a Wrap: Writing Effective Conclusions

In this Chapter
~ Why conclusions can be tricky
~ A psychological basis for strong conclusions
~ Five types of conclusions and how to write them

It's time now to wrap up the first draft of your first lifewriting feature. A good conclusion will give your feature a sense of completeness and leave your reader satisfied in the sense that, yes, it was worth taking the time to read this essay because he or she learned something important, and had an enjoyable time doing it!

Why Conclusions Can Be Tricky

Let's start with the term "conclusion," itself. A conclusion for a lifewriting feature is not the same thing as one for a problem-to-solution or effects-to-cause analytical article, which is more idea-centered than people-centered. Lifewriting emphasizes people. Even if the subject matter isn't strictly biographical, lifewriters place emphasis on the way people experience the world, not on abstract ideas in and of themselves. Hence, what "concludes" is not so much the solution to a problem as it is to what people have done to solve the problem.

A Psychological Basis for Strong Conclusions

Readers derive psychological satisfaction from features that provide what is known as "closure"—a sense of having come full circle, of loose ends having been tied (or at least the effort of tying loose ends having been made). Our need for closure probably stems from our need to capture the essence of the topic in a succinct summation—which also conveys a sense of completeness. Closure also speaks to the philosopher in all of us, that person in us who craves a parting nugget of insight, who wishes to derive as much meaning as possible from the experiences of others, and to the artist in all of us, who craves symmetry, whereby the ending returns us to the beginning, but with a deeper understanding that allows us to appreciate the wisdom only implied at the outset, but now made explicit.

Five Types of Conclusions and How to Write Them

Every stage of the writing process presents you with options, and the concluding segment of an essay is no exception. As you gain experience writing essays, you'll intuitively know what kind of conclusion will work best for you—just as experienced chefs will know just what kind of sauce or garnish to use for their prize dishes. But until you gain that level of experience, it might be helpful for you to be aware of the different types of conclusions at your disposal. Here are five common ones:

- The essential lesson learned
- A look to the future
- A parting insight or illustration of the premise
- A call to action
- Saving the best point or example for last

The Essential Lesson Learned

If your essay presents a lesson or a learning experience of some sort, then a logical and effective way to conclude would be to express, in succinct and vivid language, the essence of that lesson or experience. Common to personal experience essays, this type of ending gives you a chance to explain why the harrowing white-water rafting experience along the Snake River was more than just blind folly—that it taught you endurance and the ability to control an extremely difficult set of variables.

William Cronon, in his essay, "The Trouble With Wilderness," in which he argues that "wilderness" is less of a mythic realm and more of a human creation than we realize, concludes by conveying the essence of his premise:

> Learning to honor the wild—learning to remember and acknowledge the autonomy of the Other—means striving for critical self-consciousness in all our actions. It means that deep reflection and respect must accompany each act of [land] use, and means too that we must always consider the possibility of nonuse. It means looking at the part of nature we intend to turn toward our own ends and asking whether we can use it again and again and again—sustainably—without its being diminished in the process. It means never imagining that we can flee into a mythical wilderness to escape history and the obligation to take responsibility for our own actions that history inescapably entails. Most of all, it means practicing remembrance and gratitude, for thanksgiving is the simplest and most basic of ways to recollect the nature, the culture, and the history that have come together to make the world as we know it. If wildness can...start being as humane as it is natural, then perhaps we can get on with the unending task of struggling to live rightly in the world—not just in the garden, not just in the wilderness, but in the home that encompasses them both.
>
> William Cronon, "The Trouble With Wilderness," from *The Best American Essays*, 1996, edition. Geoffrey C. Ward (ed.). Boston: Houghton Mifflin, 1996. Originally published in *Environmental History*.

A Look to the Future

Essays that focus on the state of a current problem, such as the imminent closure of a century-old theater due to lack of funds, might end with a dual vision of the future: one in which the theater is shut down and razed, taking with it a rich cultural legacy—and one in which the theater is saved, and how its ongoing existence could enrich the community's image as an important performing-arts center in the years to come.

In his renowned (and at the time controversial) "Divinity School Address," originally delivered before Harvard's graduating divinity students in 1838, Ralph Waldo Emerson implored the graduates to ensure that one's faith "should blend with the light of rising and of setting suns, with the flying cloud, the singing bird, and the breath of flowers," and "dare to love God without mediator or veil." This is how he concludes his address:

> I look for the hour when that supreme Beauty, which ravished the souls of those Eastern men, and chiefly of those Hebrews, and through their lips spoke oracles to all time, shall speak in the West also …. I look for the new Teacher, [who] shall follow so far those shining laws, that he shall see them come full circle … shall see the world to be the mirror of the soul; shall see the identity of the law of gravitation with the purity of heart; and shall show that the Ought, that Duty, is one thing with Science, with Beauty, and with Joy.

Such an eloquent prophetic vision made for the ideal conclusion to an address that aimed to persuade these young American clergymen to break free of the antiquated views of blind servitude, to give spiritual leadership in the same sense of forging a revolutionary new vision for the new nation.

A Parting Insight or Illustration of the Premise

There are different approaches to this kind of conclusion. One is to drop clues, or little insights into the topic, and then finish off dramatically with a grand, sweeping insight. Another is to present your topic as a kind of puzzle to be solved, with the revelation disclosed at the end.

In an uncanny little essay titled "The Female Body," the novelist Margaret Atwood satirically describes a fundamental gender difference: A women is inclined to feel integrated with the world, while a man tends to feel disconnected from it—yet ironically a man tries to control a woman by compelling her to disconnect from the world in one way or another. Unable to convey his feelings of isolation a man wanders off, "not just alone, but Alone, lost in the dark ... searching for the twin who could complete him." Atwood concludes her essay as follows:

> Then it comes to him: he's lost the Female Body! Look, it shines in the gloom, far ahead, a vision of wholeness, ripeness, like a giant melon....
>
> Catch it. Put it in a pumpkin, in a high tower, in a compound, in a chamber, in a house, in a room. Quick, stick a leash on it, a lock, a chain, some pain, settle it down, so it can never get away from you again.
>
> Margaret Atwood, *Good Bones and Simple Murders*. New York: Doubleday, 1983.

Atwood's conclusion serves to illustrate the premise in a way that captures the folly of the male impulse to control women—as if controlling them will give them—the men—the illusion of feeling whole.

A Call to Action

If you write a feature that describes an exemplary way of doing something, you may want to conclude by urging your readers to follow suit, as Rufus Griscom does at the end of his piece about online dating:

Why Are Online Personals So Hot?

> Twenty years from now, the idea that someone looking for love won't look for it online will be silly, akin to skipping the card catalog to instead wander the stacks because "the right books are found only by accident." We will be charmed, but helpless to point out that the approach isn't very pragmatic. After all, how likely is it that the book of your dreams will just fall off the shelf and into your arms?

It's happened before: Monster and HotJobs rationalized the labor markets; eBay streamlined the collector markets. Online personals—which fundamentally sell people access to one another—are just now generating the kind of growth metrics witnessed at the height of the dotcom frenzy. Dating and mating will never be the same.

I stumbled upon the online dating phenomenon after cofounding *Nerve.com*—a literary magazine with a personals section that became, almost by accident, a happening singles scene. The service now doubles in size every five months; a million people have signed on in the past year and a half alone. And it's not just my company. According to Jupiter Media Metrix, between November 2001 and April 2002, the online personals market grew 29 percent to 18.6 million users—a whopping 20 percent of the singles population.

More interesting and perhaps more telling than the growth rate is who's driving it. The people signing up at *Nerve* are, by and large, young, overeducated professionals. Newly minted doctors, lawyers, journalists, and media executives are flocking to these systems, and recently we saw an ad from our first Victoria's Secret model (she actually wrote, "If you wear J. Crew, don't bother to contact me"). Whereas the short format of print lent itself to desperate, transactional relationships, (DJM SEEKS BI-CURIOUS SWF), the endless space afforded online personals is perfect for the legions of smarties who cruise there. They can show off their fancy language skills and quickly cut through a broad pool with Boolean searches. After all, things are left to chance when people don't have the tools to find what they are looking for.

But most fascinating are the new courtship patterns the medium is creating. Eighteen months ago, traffic in our system was strongest on weekdays, with daily peaks at lunch and between 5 and 6 P.M.; now it surges on Thursdays and Fridays, with hits climbing throughout the day to a first peak at around 5:30 P.M., followed by a second between 11 and midnight. What we are seeing is that browsing e-personals is becoming a social activity in itself. Furthermore, women pay to contact men as often as the reverse, which is quite different from behavior in, for example, telephone-based dating systems. It's more evidence that the virtual dating world (like the more traditional bar, nightclub, and party) is a social environment—and not just the means to an end.

In 20 years we'll look back fondly on this era as the gilded age of 21st Century dating, a computer-enabled love-letter renaissance. Alexander Graham Bell certainly meant the lovers no harm, but his invention has taken a toll on romance. By the same token, it's safe to assume that the federal government had no romantic agenda when it launched the Arpanet, the Internet's precursor. At this point in their short history, online personals are long on wit and charm, the breeding ground for a reinvigorated epistolary tradition. For now, the literate have the run of the place. So get in there while you can, because early next year, our instant-messaging client will have video capability. Technology marches on, thank goodness. But live video is likely to make the online dynamic a little more like the offline one, with cheerleaders and jocks reascendant.

While you're at it, reread Mr. Griscom's piece for its skillful use of bodybuilding strategies (statistics, description, quotation, etc.) discussed in the previous chapter.

Saving the Best Point or Example for Last

This is probably the ideal kind of conclusion for short pieces, where anything more elaborate would seem out of balance. You're concluding in the sense of ending on a dramatic note, as the following bizarre and delightful little piece by Liesl Schillinger illustrates:

Kyle Jarrow is twenty-three years old and bears a passing resemblance to Dennis the Menace. He is the kind of person who enjoys provoking people, and who can enlist a piano and a trumpet to get his point across loudly, if he wishes. His usual collaborator is an old Yale classmate, Alex Timbers, who runs a theatre company called Les Frères Corbusier. One project on their drawing board is a Scientology Christmas pageant that will star child actors and raise troubling questions about Gerhard Schröder's Germany. At the moment, however, they are engrossed in a more urgent project: the enshrinement of August 2nd as a national day of mourning.

On that day in 1923, the dashing, dissolute President Warren Gamaliel Harding—the handsomest of all American Presidents, historians concur—died suddenly, in San Francisco. In the rock opera "President Harding Is a Rock Star" (now playing in SoHo), for which Jarrow wrote the music and the lyrics, and which Timbers directed, the twenty-ninth President is subjected to the "Behind the Music" treatment. In 1920, on his fifty-fifth birthday, Harding, a not very bright schoolteacher, newspaperman, and insurance salesman from Marion, Ohio, won the Presidency in a landslide. By his fifty-eighth birthday, he had reportedly staked and lost the White House china in a poker game, his cronies had used the nation's naval oil reserves to line their own pockets (a scrape that became known as Teapot Dome), he had trysted with at least one young woman in the Oval Office, and worse, he had died. Some say he contracted a fatal case of food poisoning after eating bad crab; others say he suffered a coronary embolism or an aneurysm; still others say he was poisoned by his wife, Flossie, who had had enough of his bad behavior. But, as Flossie did not permit an autopsy, this last theory is mere conjecture.

"The current thinking is, he had an aneurysm or a stroke," says Robert Rupp, a Harding historian at West Virginia Wesleyan College and the creator of the 1993 documentary, "The Front Porch President: Warren G. Harding." "There were heart problems in his family, and, if you look at his face in photographs in the few weeks before he died, you can see that he looked terrible."

Jarrow is unconvinced. His version of Harding's demise combines two of the prevailing theories: Mrs. Harding intentionally poisoned her husband with bad crab. "Think about it," he says. "A lot of historians said it was coronary thrombosis, but, for all I know, that's the most common way that ptomaine poisoning ends up killing you! Come on! Flossie was alone with him when he died."

The playwright and the professor may never be reconciled about the cause of Harding's death, but the President's reputation is improving. To mark the eightieth anniversary of the death, Rupp will hold a symposium in Harding's home town this month. Meanwhile, in SoHo, Kyle Jarrow and his crew will celebrate the anniversary by offering their audience a crab buffet. "We will serve the pre-plucked crab that you buy in plastic containers; we'll lay it out on garnish," he said. "My feeling is there's something grotesque, in a good way, about eating naked crab before going into a musical in which you watch somebody die eating crab." In the play, Flossie Harding darts in and out, spoon-feeding her husband white, puffy chunks of crab that are actually wadded up pieces of wet white bread. ("We wanted to use real crab, but it was disgusting. He couldn't perform with the crab taste in his mouth," Jarrow said.) Toward the end, a giant crab draws the president into a crustacean danse macabre. "I feel sure it's the crab that got Harding," Jarrow said. "And, honestly, the image of an American president being chased around the stage by a giant crab is very symbolic in the way that an aneurysm isn't."

The hilarious moment in Jarrow's play about President Harding—when a giant crab draws Harding "into a crustacean danse macabre" to illustrate the theory that our 29th president had died from bad crab rather than from an aneurysm—Liesl Schillinger cleverly delays until the end of the last paragraph for maximum comic effect.

EXERCISE

Pull out the draft of one of your lifewriting essays and write a new type of conclusion for it, drawing from one of the five types discussed in this chapter, and revise any preceding part of the essay as needed to bring it in conformity with the new conclusion. Afterwards, ask yourself: Am I satisfied with this new conclusion? With the new version of the essay that this new conclusion required? Perhaps you will wish to stick with the original conclusion, but at least you will have had the experience of trying out other options.

10

Revision: The Fine Art of Reseeing Your First Draft

In this Chapter
~ The inevitability of revising
~ The flowers of afterthought
~ A method of revising
~ Preparing the second draft
~ Working with a first reader

Finishing a draft of an essay is quite an accomplishment, and you have every right to celebrate. But a finished draft does not a finished essay make, no matter how enamored you may be of it. In fact, the more enamored you are of your first draft, the less critical you're likely to be of it. The best thing to do is turn to another project and return to the draft in a few days, when you've accumulated some objectivity. Experienced writers know that a first draft is still a work in progress. You've chopped new wood, as Ezra Pound wrote in a poem addressing Walt Whitman; but now it is time for carving.

The Inevitability of Revising

The most important thing to say about revising, about carving that new, rough wood, is that it is both inevitable and pleasurable—inevitable because it's scarcely possible (nor advisable) to tend to the detail-work while you're fleshing out the big picture, pleasurable because the anxiety of laying the groundwork, of creating text out of thin air, is essentially behind you, and you may now comfortably turn to the detail work without worrying about losing sight of the big picture.

The Flowers of Afterthought

Also, rewriting activates a facet of thinking that lies dormant much of the time. Let's call it *afterthought*—the thinking that is kindled by earlier thinking, i.e., by writing that is already on the page. One of my favorite quotations about revision comes from the novelist Bernard Malamud: "I love the flowers of afterthought," he said. Let's think about the implications of that statement. Malamud is implying that a first draft represents forethought, a writer's first effort to transform ideas and impressions into language. We produce plants with buds, but it is only during revision that we transform those buds into blossoms. Revision is the fulfillment of potential. For this reason, you never want to revise hastily. Allow your flowers of afterthought to reach full bloom!

A Method of Revising

Revising, like writing a first draft, can be accomplished with greater efficiency if you exercise patience and if you follow a method. Let's start with patience. If you assume that the first draft is the "true" draft, and revising is merely correcting "mistakes," then you're going to do a rush job and overlook developmental and organizational problems that require a substantive revamping of the draft.

Resign yourself to the inevitability of revision, then take a deep breath and devote as much, if not more, time to revising as you did to the initial drafting.

I will describe my own method of revising in the following pages, but feel free to adapt this method to suit your own inclinations. My method consists of five stages:

1. Establishing critical distance
2. Reassessing the outline and treatment
3. Reading over the draft (holistic)
4. Rereading (critical) for substance, structure and coherence, accompanied by marginal annotations of hard copy
5. Preparing the second draft.

Notice that I said *second* draft, not final draft. Once you complete the new draft, I urge you to set it aside for a couple of days or more (to regain critical distance), and repeat the above stages. Do not get impatient with yourself if you keep finding things to revise even after a third or fourth draft. Revising has nothing to do with "not getting it right"—as a matter of fact, the opposite is true; the more experience you gain as a writer, the more demanding your standards will (and should) become. I've revised most of the chapters in this book five or more times. Heck, if it took Leo Tolstoy seven drafts to get *War and Peace* the way he wanted it, I've got nothing to complain about. (Tolstoy lived in a time before typewriters, let alone computers. Alas, it was Mrs. Tolstoy who did the actual transcribing. Imagine the bouts of writer's cramp she must have endured!)

Establishing Critical Distance

The first thing I do when I finish a draft is to stop thinking about it for a while. Usually, "a while" means a day or two, although sometimes, if I'm facing a deadline, I'll wait just a few hours—but that is not ideal. It's best to spend at least a day away from the draft. I may read something unrelated to what I've been working on. I may reintroduce myself to my wife. I may turn my attention to other writing projects (usually I have three or more going at once—a good writer's block preventative, by the way: When reaching a momentary impasse on one project, skip to another). Psychologists refer to this stage in the creative process as the "incubation period." The idea here is to acquire sufficient distance, emotional detachment, in order to regard the draft objectively and critically.

Now, if you compose your drafts directly at the keyboard as I often do, it is tempting to revise as you go along—and I sometimes do. This is okay, but be careful; if you start revising too soon, you'll lose momentum, which is not a good thing when trying to flesh out a first draft. Revise like this only when you feel very strongly that something is not right and that you can set things right very quickly. In the past, I would put so much time and energy into getting my opening paragraph perfect, I'd be too mentally drained to move the essay forward.

Reassessing the Outline and Treatment

The first thing you should do, as soon as you feel ready to approach your completed first draft with a cool, objective eye, is reread your outline and treatment. You want to have the essential idea and structure of your feature clear in your mind. Reconsider your premise, the way you have laid out the key aspects of the premise. It is not too late to rework these fundamental elements if a nagging inner voice is telling you that you might arrange things differently, or add new aspects of the premise—or take out old ones.

Reading (holistic)

Even before you do a first read-through of the draft, you may already be aware of some revision tasks to tend to as a result of reviewing your outline and treatment. But hold off—don't start revising until you've read through the draft *holistically*—that is, non-analytically, more as a reader than as a critic. You're letting intuition rather than intellect fan the flames at the moment. At this point, ask yourself three questions:

1. Does the draft feel complete?

2. Does the draft seem coherent? That is, does one part of it build clearly on what precedes and pave the way for what follows?

3. Does anything seem to be missing? This is a key concern in revision. Lots of things can be missing, such as the following:

• Enough body material: examples, quotations, sufficiently detailed descriptions, etc. (you may want to review Chapter 8)

• A sufficiently engaging opening that introduces your topic (review Chapter 7)

> • A conclusion that brings your essay to a satisfying close (review Chapter 9)
>
> • A solid structure in which the essay moves smoothly and logically from one point or incident to the next (review Chapter 5).

At this "holistic" draft rereading stage, pencil in quick notes. Post-it notes are ideal for this, but always indicate page and paragraph number on each note in case it accidentally peels off. Then, when you get to the next revision stage, the "analytical" stage, you can write out detailed "Insert" passages.

By the way, matters of style (good sentence structure, accurate and appropriate diction) will be your concern at the copyediting stage, which we'll get to in Chapters 13 and 14.

Rereading (critical)

Ideally, let a day or two pass before rereading the draft. This time around, it's going to be all left-brain work, so be patient—and relentless in your self-criticism. You do not want to compromise on high standards of clarity, idea development, liveliness, richness of examples and illustrations, organization, cleverness, and overall readability. In the previous revision stage, you ought to have been scribbling revision notes to yourself in the margins, or on separate sheets of paper. Now you're going to write out these additions or alterations.

Preparing the Second Draft

There are at least two ways of approaching the actual writing of the second draft. One is to "revise from spirit," as F. Scott Fitzgerald liked to say. You tend to the preliminaries, of course, you review your outline and treatment; read over the first draft—first holistically, then critically; and then you push all that preliminary stuff out of sight and write the second draft as free-spiritedly as you did the first, letting the spirit move you.

The second way, as you may have guessed, is to keep your outline and treatment in front of you and write the second draft slowly, methodically.

Which approach is best? That depends on you—and sometimes on the nature of the project at hand. Generally, I have better luck revising from spirit, but when I'm working on books, a more methodical approach, in which I adhere to a prioritized list, makes things more manageable.

At any moment during revision, new ideas, support materials, descriptions can occur to you. It might seem frustrating at first—because it will most likely mean starting a third draft to smooth things out, but that's the nature of writing.

Working with a First Reader

In my writing classes at Santa Clara University, I have students work in small groups to serve as first readers for one another's drafts. For young, beginning writers, this can be an intimidating experience—but it's an essential one. Writing, virtually by definition, means writing for others. To *publish* your work means, literally, to make it public. Inexperienced writers are skittish about showing their drafts to their peers for two main reasons: Either they're convinced their writing sucks (as they love to put it), or they're too embarrassed to share their intimate feelings and views with other students. How do I put them at ease or at least lighten their anxiety? By pointing out to them ahead of time that a draft is still a *work-in-progress*, still unfinished, and that one's intimate feelings and views, alas, are one of the biggest reasons people like to read essays, novels, and poetry. Writers simply must learn to share the deepest parts of themselves. Of course, any topics that are private should go into a private diary, not into essays for public consumption—until the author feels ready to share them with others.

The goal in reading drafts is not to evaluate them, but to respond to them strictly as readers. In other words, first readers will ask questions that the writing generates: In what way did the stranger seem threatening to you? What does this person look like? Or talk like? What went through your mind when he pulled out a knife?

Keep in mind that some of the reader-feedback you'll receive you can take or leave. Some suggestions just won't seem appropriate. Usually, a light will flash when a suggestion is right on the money—quite likely because you had already thought of it, if only semiconsciously.

A Prompt Sheet for Your First Reader

Dear Reader: This draft represents a work-in-progress. It still needs a lot of work, and your feedback will help me pinpoint specific problems with content, organization, and overall readability.

1. Does the opening paragraph engage your attention quickly and set the stage for what follows? Is there anything I should include or exclude or rearrange to strengthen the opening?

2. Are any of my assertions, descriptions, or explanations unclear or fragmentary? If so, please specify where you think greater clarity or development is needed.

3. Did I include enough examples, or different kinds of examples, to make my point(s) more convincing? Where do you think additional examples would be useful?

4. Does something seem missing from the draft? Should I bring in other people, or describe existing people more fully or depict them more dramatically?

5. Do I move logically and smoothly from one point or one scene to the next?

6. Do the people I describe come through in sufficient detail?

7. Is my conclusion satisfying? Does it wrap up loose ends? Does it provide readers with a sense of the underlying purpose or lesson learned?

8. Is the writing lively and concise? Are my sentences engaging? Where does the essay seem to "bog down"?

EXERCISES

1. Choose an entry from your daybook and develop it into a three-page mini-essay. Wait a day or two, then revise it, using the method described above. If you wish, wait two or three days after that and write a third draft. In each case, keep a careful record of all the revision techniques that you use.

2. Dig out the draft of an essay you wrote a while back, read it over a couple of times, then set it aside and "revise from spirit." Once you've completed the revision, look back at the old draft and make any changes you deem necessary. Wait a couple days, then revise it once again.

3. Keep a "revision log" of the next essay you write. Record everything you do in the way of revising—from interrupting yourself during first-draft composing to reworking the outline (or treatment) to maintaining a record of progress for each subsequent draft. Afterwards, review your log and determine whether your method of revising could be conducted more efficiently.

Part Three

Lifewriting Projects

11

Writing a Personal-Experience Feature

In this Chapter
~ The art of personal experience narration: an overview
~ Writing the personal crisis narrative
~ Writing the adventure narrative
~ Writing the return to childhood narrative

Everyone loves a good story, true or fictional. In either instance, the reader wants to know: What will happen next? How is this all going to turn out? We seem to be wired for storytelling, to experience stories vicariously—that is, to put ourselves into a story and experience in our imaginations what the narrator is experiencing.

The Art of Personal Experience Storytelling: an Overview
With personal experience narrative, nonfiction comes closest to fiction. The only difference, of course, is that a fictional experience is one that *could* have happened but was imagined instead. Keep in mind that readers, let alone editors, are not naïve about the distinction. Good personal-experience writers will include enough details—real names of real

people and places, for example—to enable readers to verify the authenticity if they're so inclined.

Let's take a close look at three popular kinds of personal experience pieces: the personal crisis narrative, the outdoor adventure narrative, and the return to childhood narrative.

Writing the Personal Crisis Narrative

We have all experienced crises of one sort or another—but what makes one worth writing about? Simply this: An important lesson was learned (personally, publicly, or both) or an ultimate good arose from the experience. You are probably familiar with several personal-crisis narratives.

In 1952, Lillian Hellman, one of America's most distinguished playwrights (*The Children's Hour*; *The Little Foxes*), was ordered before the notorious House Un-American Activities Committee, headed by Senator Joe McCarthy. Many distinguished actors and writers had been so ordered, and many captured the shameful ordeal through fiction or fictional drama (think of Arthur Miller's *The Crucible*), but few captured the experience in a book-length memoir the way Hellman did (*Scoundrel Time*, 1976).

When he was a young teenager, the African-American poet Lanston Hughes (1902–1967) describes a crisis of faith when, in church, everyone was persuading him to come forward and be saved. First read this delightful essay, taken from Hughes's autobiography *The Big Sea* (1940), for the sheer enjoyment of it. Then read it again, this time paying close attention to the way the author moves the story forward. Finally, study the analysis that follows the essay.

Salvation

I was saved from sin when I was going on thirteen. But not really saved. It happened like this. There was a big revival at my Auntie Reed's church. Every night for weeks there had been much preaching, singing, praying, and shouting, and some very hardened sinners had been brought to Christ, and the membership of the church had grown by leaps and bounds. Then just before the revival ended, they held a special meeting for children, "to bring the young lambs to the fold." My aunt spoke of it for days ahead. That night I was escorted to the front row and placed on the mourners' bench with all the other young sinners, who had not yet been brought to Jesus.

My aunt told me that when you were saved you saw a light, and something Happened to you inside! And Jesus came into your life! And God was with you from then on! She said you could see and hear and feel Jesus in your soul. I believed her. I had heard a great many old people say the same thing and it seemed to me they ought to know. So I sat there calmly in the hot, crowded church, waiting for Jesus to come to me.

The preacher preached a wonderful rhythmical sermon, all moans and shouts and lonely cries and dire pictures of hell, and then he sang a song about the ninety and nine safe in the fold, but one little lamb was left out in the cold. Then he said, "Won't you come? Won't you come to Jesus? Young lambs, won't you come?"

And he held out his arms to all us young sinners there on the mourners' bench. And the little girls cried. And some of them jumped up and went to Jesus right away. But most of us just sat there.

A great many older people came and knelt around us and prayed, old women with jet-black faces and braided hair, old men with work-gnarled hands. And the church sang a song about the lower lights are burning, some poor sinners to be saved. And the whole building rocked with prayer and song.

Still I kept waiting to *see* Jesus.

Finally all the young people had gone to the altar and were saved, but one boy and me. He was a rounder's [i.e., a drunkard's] son named Westley. Westley and I were surrounded by sisters and deacons praying. It was very hot in the church, and getting late now. Finally Westley said to me in a whisper: "God damn! I'm tired o' sitting here. Let's go up and be saved." So he got up and was saved.

Then I was left all alone on the mourners' bench. My aunt came and knelt at my knees and cried, while prayers and songs swirled all around me in the little church. The whole congregation prayed for me alone, in a mighty wail of moans and voices. And I kept waiting serenely for Jesus, waiting—but he didn't come. I wanted to see him, but nothing happened to me. Nothing! I wanted something to happen to me, but nothing happened.

I heard the songs and the minister saying: "Why don't you come? My dear child, why don't you come to Jesus? Jesus is waiting for you. He wants you. Why don't you come? Sister Reed, what is this child's name?"

"Langston," my aunt sobbed.

"Langston, why don't you come? Why don't you come and be saved? Oh, Lamb of God! Why don't you come?"

Now it was really getting late. I began to be ashamed of myself, holding everything up so long. I began to wonder what God thought about Westley, who certainly hadn't seen Jesus either, but who was now sitting proudly on the platform, swinging his knickerbockered legs and grinning down at me, surrounded by deacons and old women on their knees praying. God had not struck Westley dead for taking his name in vain or lying in the temple. So I decided that maybe to save further trouble, I'd better lie, too, and say that Jesus had come, and get up and be saved

So I got up.

Suddenly the whole room broke into a sea of shouting, as they saw me rise. Waves of rejoicing swept the place. Women leaped in the air. My aunt threw her arms around me. The minister took me by the hand and led me to the platform.

When things quieted down, in a hushed silence, punctuated by a few ecstatic "Amens," all the new young lambs were blessed in the name of God. Then joyous singing filled the room.

That night, for the last time in my life but one—for I was a big boy twelve years old—I cried. I cried, in bed alone, and couldn't stop. I buried my head under the quilts, but my aunt heard me. She woke up and told my uncle I was crying because the Holy Ghost had come into my life, and because I had seen Jesus. But I was really crying because I couldn't bear to tell her that I had lied, that I had deceived everybody in the church, and I hadn't seen Jesus, and that now I didn't believe there was a Jesus any more, since he didn't come to help me.

Langston Hughes, "Salvation," from *The Big Sea*. New York: Hill & Wang, 1940.

Hughes has carefully structured his narrative so that we keep wondering to the end whether young Langston is going to give in to the pressure and come forward, or not. Notice how Hughes manages to make his readers vicariously experience the pressure to submit, the incessant pleading from the minister and the relatives, and ultimately from the entire congregation; the hot, stifling church, the feelings of guilt. Notice, too, how Hughes *sustains* the drama: As the members of the congregation press Langston to come forward and be saved, the boy's resistance gradually erodes. If Hughes had simply bypassed the drama with a summative sentence like, "After constant cajoling, I finally gave in and stepped forward," the scene would not have been nearly so memorable.

Always keep in mind, when developing your own narratives, that the greatest pleasure in reading a narrative essay is being caught up in the drama. If you resolve matters too quickly, the reader will be disappointed.

Writing the Adventure Narrative

It seems that readers cannot get enough of true adventure stories. As our professional lives get busier and busier, we hunger for escape through adventure. Many of us, myself included, have a bit of Indiana Jones in our blood—ready to seek out the long-lost treasure, braving amazing obstacles from snake dens to ancient curses to Nazis along the way.

An adventure narrative follows essentially the same structure as its fictional counterpart, you unfold the story along a rising curve of suspense, of conflict, until a crisis is reached, followed by a climax in which the conflict is resolved, followed by a denouement (a fancy word for resolution). Note how Mark Twain uses this narrative pattern in the following passage from *Roughing It* (1872), which focuses on one of his prospecting adventures in Nevada during the 1860s:

> I confess, without shame, that I expected to find masses of silver lying all about the ground. I expected to see it glittering in the sun on the mountain summits ....
>
> The first opportunity that offered, I sauntered carelessly away from the cabin, keeping an eye on the other boys, and stopping and contemplating the sky when they seemed to be observing me; but as soon as the coast was manifestly clear, I fled away as guiltily as a thief might have done and never halted till I was far beyond sight and call. Then I began my search with a feverish excitement that was brimful of expectation—almost of certainty. I crawled about the ground, seizing and examining bits of stone, blowing the dust from them or rubbing them on my clothes, and then peering at them with anxious hope. Presently I found a bright fragment and my heart bounded! I hid behind a boulder and polished it and scrutinized it with a nervous eagerness and a delight that was more pronounced than absolute certainty itself could have afforded. The more I examined the fragment the more I was convinced that I had found the door to fortune. I marked the spot and carried away my specimen. Up and down the rugged mountain side I searched, with always increasing interest and always augmenting gratitude that I had come to Humboldt and come in time. Of all the experiences of my life, this secret search among the hidden treasures of silver-land was the nearest to unmarred ecstasy. It was a delirious revel. By and by, in the bed of a shallow rivulet, I found a deposit of shining yellow scales, and my breath almost

forsook me! A gold mine, and in my simplicity I had been content with vulgar silver!

… As I walked along I could not help smiling at the thought of my being so excited over my fragment of silver when a nobler metal was almost under my nose. In this little time the former had so fallen in my estimation that once or twice I was on the point of throwing it away.

[Twain soon learns, when he returns to the others, that his little treasure was just a worthless piece of granite; that gold—and even silver—was much more difficult to come upon than he ever imagined.]

True knowledge of the nature of silver mining came fast enough …. We climbed the mountain sides, and clambered among sagebrush, rocks and snow till we were ready to drop with exhaustion, but found no silver—nor yet any gold.

Day after day we did this. Now and then we came upon holes burrowed a few feet into the declivities and apparently abandoned; and now and then we found a few listless men still burrowing. But there was no appearance of silver. These holes were the beginnings of tunnels, and the purpose was to drive them hundreds of feet into the mountain, and some day tap the hidden ledge where the silver was.

Some day! It seemed far enough away, and very hopeless and dreary. Day after day we toiled, and climbed and searched, and we younger partners grew sicker and still sicker of the promiseless toil. At last we halted under a beetling rampart of rock which projected from the earth high upon the mountain.

Mr. Ballou broke off some fragments with a hammer, and examined them long and attentively with a small eye-glass; threw them away and broke off more; said this rock was quartz, and quartz was the sort of rock that contained silver.

Contained it! I had thought that at least it would be caked on the outside of it like a kind of veneering. He still broke off pieces and critically examined them, now and then wetting the piece with his tongue and applying the glass. At last he exclaimed:

"We've got it!"

We were full of anxiety in a moment. The rock was clean and white, where it was broken, and across it ran a ragged thread of blue. He said that that little thread had silver in it, mixed with base metals, such as lead and antimony, and other rubbish, and that there was a speck or two of gold visible. After a great deal of effort we managed to discern some little fine yellow specks, and judged that a couple of tons of them massed together might make a gold dollar, possibly.

Twain uses his naïve optimism about discovering a mother-lode of silver, then gold, as the energy driving the narrative forward; so as the reader keeps wondering when the big discovery will come, Twain is meanwhile conveying (in his inimitable, colloquial manner) an important lesson about prospecting: The disappointments far outweigh the successes.

Writing the Return to Childhood Narrative

All of us revisit our childhood past now and then. We might do so out of nostalgia for a time in our lives less burdened by responsibility, more magical, more filled with possibilities, but we might also dwell upon our childhood years for more practical reasons: to revisit the origins of a current state of affairs, to rethink the time when our lives began to change for one reason or another.

In her essay, "Beauty: When the Other Dancer Is the Self," Alice Walker recalls a time when playing cowboys and Indians with her two brothers ended with a terrible accident:

I am eight years old and a tomboy. I have a cowboy hat, cowboy boots, checkered shirt and pants, all red. My playmates are my brothers, two and four years older than I.... On Saturday nights we all go to the picture show, even my mother; Westerns are her favorite kind of movie. Back home, "on the ranch,"... we chase each other for hours rustling cattle, being outlaws, delivering damsels from distress. Then my parents decide to buy my brothers guns. These are not "real" guns. They shoot BBs, copper pellets my brothers say will kill birds. Because I am a girl, I do not get a gun. Instantly I am relegated to the position of Indian....

One day while I am standing on top of our makeshift "garage"—pieces of tin nailed across some poles—holding my bow and arrow and looking out toward the fields, I feel an incredible blow in my right eye. I look down just in time to see my brother lower his gun.

Both brothers rush to my side. My eye stings, and I cover it with my hand. "If you tell," they say, "we will get a whipping. You don't want that to happen, do you?" I do not. "Here is a piece of wire," says the older brother, picking it up from the roof; "say you stepped on one end of it and the other flew up and hit you." The pain is beginning to start. "Yes," I say. "Yes, I will say that is what happened."

Confronted by our parents we stick to the lie agreed upon. They place me on a bench on the porch and I close my left eye while they examine the right. There is a tree growing from underneath the porch that climbs past the railing to the roof. It is the last thing my right eye sees. I watch as its trunk, its branches, and then its leaves are blotted out by the rising blood.

Alice Walker, from *In Search of Our Mothers' Gardens: Womanist Prose.* Harcourt, 1974.

Notice how Walker is able to bring the reader—and herself—back to this fateful day, with just one sentence: "I am eight years old and a tomboy." With the next few sentences we're in that child's play-world—but very quickly the complications of the adult world intrude: "Then my parents decide to buy my brothers guns." The irony is razor sharp here. The children did not need guns because they could easily pretend they already had them when they played cowboys and Indians. And, notice how cleverly Walker doubles that irony with the next sentence: "They are not 'real' guns." No, not in the sense that they used bullets, but real enough with their use of BBs, to inflict terrible harm.

Each of us, I would argue, has had childhood experiences that are worth writing about. They do not have to be about bad things happening, like losing an eye—they could be about something relatively innocuous, like reading a particular book, that set your life on a new course. Readers benefit greatly from reading about such childhood experiences.

EXERCISES

1. Use your daybook to write mini-narratives about personal ordeals you've recently experienced. Don't make the mistake of overlooking an ordeal as not worth writing about; one never knows whether an experience worth writing an essay about until enough time for perspective has passed. You might prove this to yourself by returning to some of these mini-narratives a month down the road, and developing them into full-fledged lifewriting features.

2. The next time you embark on an outdoor adventure—skiing, hiking in the woods, a hot-air balloon ride, cycling across the state—take your pocket notebook with you and resolve to fill it with detailed notes of your outing. Take photographs to supplement the moments. As soon as you return home, begin working your notes into a narrative.

3. Open a new document on your computer and take a spontaneous trip down memory lane, pausing at various moments in your childhood from, say, age 5 through age 12. Write quickly, focusing only on the details of the memory, not on the manner of narration. Afterwards, choose one of these spontaneous narratives and work it into a full-fledged essay.

4. Try your hand at a personal narrative that combines a crisis with an adventure—or with a return to childhood. For example, you might write about the time, one winter afternoon, when you and a friend went hiking in the woods—against your parents' wishes (adventure), but then got stuck in a blizzard (crisis).

12

Writing Portraits and Self-Portraits

In this Chapter
~ The art of literary portraiture: an overview
~ Writing a single-subject portrait
~ Writing a group portrait
~ Writing a self portrait

Nonfiction of any kind, aside from the specialized technical stuff, is directly or indirectly about people; that's why the possibilities for lifewriting are so vast. This chapter, though, focuses on the direct type, what is conventionally referred to as biographical or autobiographical writing, but what I like to call *portrait* writing because of the association this term has with the visual arts. The association is important because good autobiographical or biographical writing enables the readers to envision the subjects as if they'd been captured by sketch artists or portrait painters.

The Art of Literary Portraiture: an Overview
Literature is replete with portraiture: Emerson's profile of his good friend Henry Thoreau (which he delivered as a eulogy at Thoreau's funeral), James Boswell's life of the great eighteenth-century lexicographer

and critic Samuel Johnson, Chaucer's colorful verse-portraits of the pilgrims and the characters in the stories they tell as they ride toward Canterbury. We can go back even farther than that—to the Greek biographer/philosopher Plutarch (A.D. 46–120), whose profiles of Greeks and Roman lawmakers like Solon, conquerers like Alexander the Great, and even dictators like Lycurgus, collected in his *Lives*, influenced authors for centuries to come because of the in-depth manner in which Plutarch portrayed his subjects, including their vices as well as virtues.

People love to read about other people for several reasons. Reading about human nature helps us deal with it better; it also sheds light on our own natures. As readers, we can better understand ideas when they're put into human contexts. Who could have imagined that a stage play based on *theoretical physics* of all subjects—I'm speaking of Michael Frayn's *Copenhagen* (1998)—could have enjoyed great success around the world? The reason is that the playwright focused on the *human drama* underlying the science: a meeting during World War II between Niels Bohr and Werner Heisenberg, the world's two foremost atomic physicists, good friends but political opponents, to discuss atomic theory. (But is Heisenberg's curiosity purely scientific or is it tainted by loyalty to the Nazi cause? That is one of the conundrums that the play considers.)

Writing a Single-Subject Portrait

We enjoy reading in depth about fascinating people. We want to know the secrets of their success, what makes these people tick. Were they born brilliant? Did they struggle to achieve their fame and fortune, or were things handed to them on the proverbial silver platter? Were they fortunate enough to have parents or teachers who recognized their genius early on and did all they could to nurture it?

Let's look at a famous example, the nurturing of the musical prodigy Wolfgang Amadeus Mozart. You probably have heard stories—or remember Milos Forman's award-winning film, *Amadeus*—about the way Mozart's father, Leopold, took his young son all over Europe to show off his prodigious musical talents. This is all true, but what isn't as certain is the degree to which Leopold influenced and instructed his son. Here is how

Maynard Solomon, a professor of music at Yale University, approaches the topic in his biographical portrait of Mozart:

> While Mozart was rapidly emerging as a composer, absorbing influences, learning a variety of styles, and working within a range of genres, Leopold was hastening him along with assistance and instruction, which often merged into a collaboration that could scarcely be acknowledged. Leopold Mozart called attention to a series of three consecutive fifths in the second minuet of the violin Sonata K.9, saying that he had corrected them but that they had been left in by an engraver's oversight and that this in turn was fortunate, for they constituted "a proof that our little Wolfgang composed them himself, which, perhaps quite naturally, everyone will not believe." Clearly he was concerned that the outside world might draw unwarranted conclusions from what was, to the Mozarts, only a manifestation of intimate cooperation within the family enterprise.
>
> Maynard Solomon, *Mozart: A Life*. New York: HarperCollins, 1995.

Solomon aims to demystify the myth of Mozart's genius and focus on the reality (insofar as that reality can be reconstructed with some degree of reliability). To be sure, Mozart was genius enough without having to perpetuate the myth that his musical ability was, as many of the spectators of the day thought, magical or supernatural.

Of course, portraiture needn't be so reportorial. It can be lighthearted, witty, or, as in the case of theater critic John Lahr's portrait of playwright David Mamet (*American Buffalo*, *Glengarry Glen Ross*, *House of Games*, etc.), intimate and based on one's own interaction with the subject:

> When I met David Mamet ... he made me the gift of a Boy Scout knife. On one side of the knife was the Scout motto: "Be prepared." The words, which invoke both prowess and paranoia, seemed to sum up the twin themes

of Mamet's work, and of his guarded life. We were sitting in the back room of his headquarters, on the second floor of a two-story yellow clapboard building on Eliot Street in Cambridge, Massachusetts, at a table with a large Second World War poster hanging over it which read "Loose Talk Can Cost Lives! Keep It Under Your Stetson." There was no identifying name on the bell to the front door or on the office door. You had to feel your way along until you found Mamet hidden away, which is how it is with him. Mamet, who is masterly at communicating his meanings in public, is prickly in private. He is a small but powerfully built man; in the stillness of his presence and in the precision of his sentences, he exudes an imposing, specific gravity. "Fortress Mamet" is how Ed Koren, the cartoonist and Mamet's Vermont neighbor, refers to the emotional no-go area that Mamet creates around himself, and I was acutely aware of this hazardous moat as Mamet eased into a chair across the table from me, wearing his summer camouflage: a khaki baseball cap, khaki shorts, and a purple-and-brown Hawaiian shirt.

John Lahr, "Fortress Mamet." *The New Yorker*, Nov. 17, 1997.

By focusing on particular details—the inscription on the Boy Scout knife—Lahr enables his readers to envision Mamet easily and at the same time uses these details as occasions to bring up more abstract aspects of Mamet's complex personality and art.

Writing a Group Portrait

Sometimes people become more interesting when described in terms of a group or organization with which they've been long associated. We may enjoy reading individual portraits of Frank Sinatra, of Dean Martin, of Sammy Davis, Jr., and of Joey Bishop—but we are equally, if not more, fascinated by their interactions as The Rat Pack.

In *Of a Fire On the Moon*, his richly textured study of the people, politics, and technology behind the historic Apollo 11 mission, Norman Mailer creates fascinating comparisons among the astronauts in the program, as in the following comparison between Neil Armstrong and Buzz Aldrin:

> They were a curious mating of opposites, a team picked most probably for their complementary abilities and aptitudes. Temperamentally they suggested the equivalent of one of those dour Vermont marriages where the bride dies after sixty years and the husband sits rocking on the farmhouse porch. "Guess you feel pretty bad, Zeb, that Abigail is gone." The chair keeps rocking, there is a long puff on the pipe. "Nope," says Zeb, "never did get to like her much."
>
> It was not a case of Armstrong and Aldrin disliking each other. How would one ever know? It is almost as if the question never occurred to them....
>
> Yet how remarkable if their personalities didn't impinge upon one another, for they were profoundly different men. Armstrong...was a virtuoso of a flyer; Aldrin was a powerful personification of organized human intelligence. Of course, he could fly a plane well, just as he could give a superior performance at any number of activities from pole vaulting to celestial mechanics, but in relation to other astronauts, he was not among the more accomplished aviators, he had not in fact even been a test pilot. Yet of all these men he was the one whose command of mathematics and complex statistical operations was so turned to the logic of information systems that he was doubtless the nearest human equivalent to a computer at NASA, and had a doctor of science degree in astronautics from MIT, the only one in the first three groups of astronauts to have earned his doctorate.
>
> Norman Mailer, *Of a Fire on the Moon*. Boston: Little, Brown, 1970.

Some might call Mailer's approach to lifewriting "quirky" in that he colors his profiles of the individual astronauts with witty, often satirical comparisons, as in comparing Armstrong and Aldrin with the imaginary Zeb and Abigail to give humorous emphasis to the way the two astronauts work closely together yet never really "bonded." The lesson here is that you, the author, need never suppress your own peculiar angle of vision, your own biases, in your own lifewriting.

Writing a Self-Portrait

Because people learn from one another, everyone is interested in one's life experiences and world views. It isn't true, as some writing teachers proclaim, that before you can start writing your memoirs, or even short features about yourself, you need to have lived through exotic or harrowing experiences. What matters is that the experiences you wish to write about be interesting and useful to others. It's not so much what you have experienced as the unusual perspective or depth of insight you have acquired from that experience. But how does one tease out these experiences? Your daybook can help you recall experiences from long ago, as well as more recent experiences that for one reason or another you've put into deep storage, thinking that no one else would find them worth reading about.

In his memoir, *Uncle Tungsten*, the neurologist and author Oliver Sacks, whose book, *Awakenings*, chronicled his work with Parkinson's Disease patients and became the basis for the Penny Marshall film starring Robin Williams and Robert DeNiro, writes about the way chemistry helped shape his boyhood, and his destiny. The first chapter begins like this:

> Many of my childhood memories are of metals: these seemed to exert a power on me from the start. They stood out, conspicuous against the heterogeneousness of the world, by their shining, gleaming quality, their silveriness, their smoothness and weight. They seemed cool to the touch, and they rang when they were struck.
>
> I loved the yellowness, the heaviness, of gold. My mother would take the wedding ring from her finger and let me handle it for a while, as she told me of its inviolacy, how it never tarnished. "Feel how heavy it is," she

would add. "It's even heavier than lead." I knew what lead was, for I had handled the heavy, soft piping the plumber had left one year. Gold was soft, too, my mother told me, so it was usually combined with another metal to make it harder.

It was the same with copper—people mixed it with tin to produce bronze. Bronze!—the very word was like a trumpet to me, for battle was the brave clash of bronze upon bronze, bronze spears on bronze shields, the great shield of Achilles....

I knew copper, the shiny rose color of the great copper cauldron in our kitchen—it was taken down only once a year, when the quinces and crab apples were ripe in the garden and my mother would stew them to make jelly.

I knew zinc: the dull, slightly bluish birdbath in the garden was made of zinc; and tin, from the heavy tinfoil in which sandwiches were wrapped for a picnic. My mother showed me that when tin or zinc was bent it uttered a special "cry." "It's due to deformation of the crystal structure," she said, forgetting that I was five, and could not understand her—and yet her words fascinated me, made me want to know more.

Oliver Sacks, *Uncle Tungsten: Memories of a Chemical Boyhood*. New York: Knopf, 2001.

I find it remarkable—do you as well?—how metals and their properties themselves contributed as much to Sacks's childhood memories as the objects of which they were made, as much as the occasions for which those objects were used, or the people who used them. The last sentence in the passage quoted above is especially revealing, not only about Sacks's childhood, but about the nature of childhood in general: When a parent rouses curiosity about the nature of things in a young child, that parent is setting precious wheels in motion: the wheels of fascination with and curiosity about the world that will continue turning for the rest of that child's life.

Whenever you write about moments in your life, stay alert for "destiny shapers," like young Oliver Sacks's mother telling him that zinc utters a special cry when you bend it because of the way its crystals are structured.

EXERCISES

1. Journey back to your earliest childhood memory—or one of your earliest. Write a page or so in your daybook describing it. Include the following:

(a) Why do you suppose you've remembered this experience for so long? What makes it so special?

(b) What physical details can you recall?

(c) What emotional details can you recall?

(d) Which individuals, if any, were part of the memory?

(e) Did the events involved in this memory shape your childhood in some way? How?

2. Keep a running list of individuals who might be good candidates for profiles. You may wish to divide the list into categories such as: Close Friends, Family Members, Coworkers, Neighbors, Athletes, Celebrities I Most Admire, People Who Rub Me the Wrong Way, and so on.

3. Write a group profile of two or more individuals who interact together yet are distinctively different from one another. Have fun highlighting the physical and/or behavioral differences.

Part Four

Developing Your Style

13

Copyediting for Style I:
Strengthening Your Sentences

In this Chapter
~ Three elements of strong sentences
~ Improving sentence coherence
~ Sentence emphasis
~ Adding sentence variety
~ Trimming the fat to improve clarity and vigor
~ How to do a self-analysis of your prose style
~ From sentence to paragraph

This chapter and the next will guide you through the methods of polishing, or more precisely, of *copyediting* the lifewriting draft you've completed. Of course, you can also study these chapters in order to practice improving your writing style generally. In addition to holistic revising to strengthen the essay's content and structure (see Chapter 10), writers copyedit their manuscripts to make them more readable—that is, they look for ways to strengthen their sentences (what we'll be focusing on in this chapter), as well as ways to improve their word usage (the focus of Chapter 14).

Three Elements of Strong Sentences

Editing sentences for readability means looking for the following elements:

1. *Coherence*: how well the sentences link up; i.e., how logically one idea flows into the next.
2. *Emphasis*: how effectively the sentence elements are arranged.
3. *Variety*: how well the sentences capture the writer's distinctive voice and personality.

Improving Sentence Coherence

The biggest contributor to readability is coherence. If one sentence doesn't lead logically to the next, or follow logically from the one before it, the writing is said to be incoherent. One way to test for this coherence is to read your sentences aloud to someone. If the listener has trouble following along, you need to reconstruct your sentences so that they give readers better clues as to how they connect. Consider the following paragraph:

> Erika and Stan enjoyed their first date together. They went to see a movie, then they ate dinner at an Italian restaurant. The movie they saw was a science-fiction movie called *Solaris*. Erika loved it. She thought it was haunting and spellbinding. But Stan disliked it because it confused him. But they did enjoy the Italian dinner.

See how disconnected the sentences are? It is as if the author were jotting things down in a haphazard, free-associative manner without regard to whether they were building upon a central idea. This is okay for daybook writing, but not for drafting. Before reading on, take a piece of scratch paper and try revising the passage, keeping this key principle in mind: *Keep related ideas together*.

Now study this coherent revision of the paragraph:

> On their first date together, Erika and Stan ate at an Italian restaurant, delighted that they both loved Italian

food, and discussed *Solaris*, the movie they had just seen. They quickly discovered that their taste in movies was quite different from their taste in food. Whereas Stan disliked the film because he found it disjointed, confusing, and "just too weird" (a problem he had with most science fiction movies), Erika loved it *because* of its weirdness, of the way it refused to fall back on those predictable Hollywood plot scenarios.

The first thing the writer did was keep the related items together—Italian food here, movie stuff there. Next, notice how the writer reworked the sentences to establish a clear *relationship* between their taste in food and their taste in movies. This relationship is not nearly as apparent in the first version.

Another important way in which sentence construction can ensure clear relationships among sentence items is known as subordination. Consider these two sentences:

It rained all afternoon. I stayed indoors.

What is the relationship between these sentences? Because it isn't explicit, readers must pause, however slightly, to make that determination. This interferes with readability. By turning two separate sentences into one sentence consisting of a subordinate clause (a clause that begins with a subordinate conjunction such as *because, when, although,* etc.), any possible ambiguity in relationship is eliminated:

Because it rained all afternoon, I stayed indoors.

But the relationship expressed could also be:

Even though it rained all afternoon, I stayed indoors.

—implying that the speaker enjoys being out in the rain.

Sentence Emphasis

Take another look at the above example. To highlight the difference between Erika's and Stan's reaction to *Solaris*, the writer chose a sentence pattern that would give the most dramatic emphasis to that difference:

> Whereas Stan disliked the film because he found it disjointed, confusing, and "just too weird" ... Erika loved it *because* of its weirdness ....

Emphasizing a point like that adds vitality to your prose.

Here's another suggestion: Place the point you wish to emphasize at the beginning or end of a sentence. Notice how the emphasis changes in the following sentences:

> During February, when it snowed for three consecutive days, I thought seriously of moving to California.

> I thought seriously of moving to California when, during February, it snowed for three consecutive days.

Always be aware of what you wish to emphasize when you construct your sentences.

Adding Sentence Variety

Variety is the spice not only of life but of sentence structure. When sentences in a paragraph are patterned too much alike, the writing seems wooden, clunky. Read the following passage about the fascination that many people have with gambling and note the way the sentences are structured:

> Thousands of people come from all over the northeastern United States to a rather desolate spot in rural Connecticut. Here, they leave $50 to $100 per person. Why do they do this? They seem to do it for nothing but the uncertain manner of making the deposit. Maybe they

also do it because it is titillating. No one is coercing these people to tax themselves. Some may come to see performances by big name stars. The stars are used as a hook for the real theater. That theater is gambling.

Do you see what the problem is? The content is good, the progression of ideas is good, yet the sentences just do not "flow," as my students like to say. In other words, the sentences move mechanically, like Frankenstein's monster, across the page: clop-clop-clop-clop-clop. They lack variety. They lack personality. Now read the passage as it was actually written:

What is it that moves many thousands of people to come from all over the northeastern United States to a rather desolate spot in rural Connecticut to leave, on average, $50 to $100 per person, in exchange for nothing but the uncertain and perhaps titillating manner of making the deposit? No one is coercing these people to tax themselves. To be sure, some may come to see performances by big-name stars. Theatrical stars are used as a hook for the real theater—that of gambling.

Karl E. Scheibe, *The Drama of Everyday Life*. Cambridge: Harvard University Press, 2000.

The first thing you probably noticed about Scheible's passage is that the sentences vary in length. In the earlier adulterated version, they're nearly all the same length. Another cause of clunkiness is lack of transitional elements. Notice how in Scheible's version a simple transitional phrase, like "to be sure," contributes to the coherence (it calls attention to the relationship between the preceding sentence and the current sentence), and to the conversational tone.

Trimming the Fat to Improve Clarity and Vigor

Wordiness can be caused by several factors. Lack of coherence is one, as we noticed in the above example about Stan and Erika. Another is simply using more words than you need to get the idea across. Consider this sentence:

> Courtesy is a gesture that people like to be shown.

The sentence is wordy because it is burdened with a useless definition ("Courtesy is a gesture"), when the point of the sentence is to explain why people like to be treated with courtesy. We can convey that with just three words:

> People appreciate courtesy.

Notice also how the first construction forces the writer to use a listless auxiliary verb ("is") rather than a strong verb ("appreciate"), which conveys the meaning much more forcefully.

Another cause of wordiness in sentences is overreliance on sluggish phrases like "there is," "there are," "that is," etc.

> There is a tendency among teenage drivers to speed.
> Bicycling is an exercise that is an effective way of toning the thighs.

Readers have to work their way six words into the first sentence to encounter the subject ("teenage drivers"). Also, "there is" forces you to rely on those weak auxiliary verbs, as well as forces you to use a noun phrase ("a tendency") that would work much better as a verb:

> Teenage drivers tend to speed.

In the second example, the subject begins the sentence, but it is cluttered by an unnecessary definition ("... is an exercise"), and a verbose explanation ("an effective way of toning the thighs"), introduced by the weak expletive ("that is"). Once you settle on a strong verb, you can convey the meaning more efficiently:

> Bicycling tones the thighs effectively.

Still another cause of wordiness is redundancy—more than one word meaning the same thing, as in *true facts* (no such thing as false facts) or *past history* (if it's not in the past, it's not history); words that are obviously implied by another word (*orange in color; free gift*) or words used for unnecessary emphasis, as in *each and every, frightened and scared, hopeful and optimistic*.

How to Do a Self-Analysis of Your Prose Style

Writing effective sentences is a relatively easy skill to master, but you do need to spend a fair amount of time becoming proficient at it. The first step is to analyze your own prose. Here is one method to do that:

1. *Read part of an essay-in-progress aloud to someone.* The next best thing is to read it aloud to yourself, foolish as you might feel. Because one of the hallmarks of a good prose style is natural rhythm, reading aloud will call attention to any rhythmic irregularities. If you find yourself stumbling with the sentences as you read them aloud, or putting in words that aren't there, or you get the feeling that you're not sounding like yourself, or if your listener complains that your tone seems artificial or mechanical or flat—then that's a good sign you need to work on your sentence construction.

2. *Circle the sentences you had trouble reading.* You'll need to keep a red pen in hand while reading your draft aloud. Whenever you stumble, or stop because the sentence doesn't seem to make sense or hold together, circle it before continuing.

3. *Rewrite the problem sentences.* Do this as soon after reading aloud as possible. And, while you're at it, try writing out several versions of these sentences, not just one. This will help you get a feel for the great flexibility of syntax, and it will increase your skill in manipulating syntactic elements. Read the new sentences aloud.

4. *Double-check for coherence, emphasis, and variety.* Sentences may seem okay in isolation, but cumbersome in the context of other sentences.

From Sentence to Paragraph

Misinformation about paragraphs abound—e.g., that all paragraphs must have a topic sentence, two or more supporting sentences, and a concluding sentence. That might be an ideal paragraph construction for certain situations, such as arguing a premise, but to apply that "rule" to all paragraphs is nonsense.

A paragraph can be just one sentence long—even one word long, if the writer wishes that kind of emphasis. Who decides how long or short a paragraph should be?

You.

See what I mean?

Such "emphasis paragraphing" should be used sparingly, otherwise your writing will seem gimmicky. For the most part, good paragraphing is marked by unity: everything relating to a central point, and making sure that central point gets emphasized—either at the beginning of the paragraph or at the end. Here is an example of each:

With the topic sentence at the beginning of the paragraph:

> Lupita is an experienced choral singer. She sang in a church choir from ages 8 to 15. During her late teens, she sang as a mezzo-soprano in the Bach Society Choir. As if that weren't enough, she appeared as a lead singer in two musicals. Just as important, she practices daily with one of the best voice teachers in the country.

The point that the topic sentence makes is exemplified by the subsequent sentences, with the last sentence being the most emphatic.

With the topic sentence at the end of the paragraph:

> I begin to forget things. I lose patience and get irritable easily, even with my best friends. My energy may remain at a high level, but it will most likely dissipate before the workday ends. Worst of all, I start to feel that I'm losing touch with my surroundings. Clearly, not getting enough sleep is a serious problem for me.

You can probably guess why the writer chose to place the topic sentence at the end: It is to heighten curiosity about the "punch line."

EXERCISES

1. Revise the following paragraphs to make the sentences in each relate to one another more coherently. You may need to add, change, or eliminate some words, as well as rework or reposition sentences for greater emphasis or variety.

(a) Milly has an interesting hobby. It is collecting antique soda-pop bottles.

Her Coca-Cola bottles date back to World War I. Her collection includes Pepsi Cola bottles, 7-Up bottles, and Dad's Root Beer bottles. Her Dr. Pepper bottles go back almost as far as her Coca-Cola bottles.

(b) Cats are fun to watch because they are so playful. They are not fun to feed because they are so finicky. Cats are peaceful creatures because they curl up and sleep a lot. It isn't always obvious but cats are intelligent. Cats are the ideal pets. They can tell when you're not feeling well. They can tell when you are going to go away.

2. Strengthen the following sluggish and wordy sentences:

(a) There were several cars along the road that had been overturned by the hurricane.

(b) Lenore was a woman who would not tolerate or put up with slipshod work in any way, shape, or form from her employees.

(c) Tomorrow we are going to have a meeting in which the President will present his argument that a major reduction of supply costs can be made.

14

Copyediting for Style II: Choosing Words Wisely

In this Chapter

~ The three principles of effective diction
~ Biased and inclusive usage: a commonsensicle approach
~ Avoiding vacant and insincere usage
~ Having fun with words or dancing with figures of speech
~ A closer look at metaphor
~ People words
~ Getting curious about word origins

Of all the tools in a writer's toolbox, words are the most basic. Your "way with words" is one of the first things an editor notices: Is your diction (word-choice) precise and suitable for the occasion? Do you value concision over verbosity? Do your words impart a liveliness and energy to your ideas that give your readers the feeling you're not only jazzed about the subject matter, but eager to have the opportunity to be sharing these ideas with them? Let's take a closer look at effective word-wielding to see how it's done.

The Three Principles of Effective Diction

1 *Use words that are part of your natural vocabulary.* Novice writers sometimes grope for impressive-sounding words, falsely assuming that readers will take them more seriously if they use highfalutin language. The opposite is true. Readers can pick up quickly on forced or staged writing. And, there is always the risk of using words erroneously and making a fool out of yourself, as sometimes happens when writers use a thesaurus to select specialized, exotic-sounding words over simpler, more appropriate words merely to sound "educated."

By the way, if you think your vocabulary is too limited, don't waste time trying to enlarge it by memorizing lists purported to increase your word power. The only sensible way to enlarge your vocabulary is to become acquainted with words in context—that is to say, simply read more. Read not only what interests you, but read to expand your interests. When you venture outside of your comfort zone of familiarity, you most often encounter unfamiliar words. If you're a writer worth your salt, you should harbor an insatiable curiosity about everything. You never know what you might find useful, regardless of the subjects you're most interested in writing about.

2. *Use words that are appropriate to the occasion*—that is, appropriate to the audience you're addressing, as well as to the subject matter. If you're writing about baby care, for example, you may safely assume that your readers are young mothers and that the language you use will be appropriate for this lay readership, and not for, say, health care professionals. Before setting out to write or even plan your lifewriting feature, read as many published features in the subject area as you can. When you study a piece, first read it quickly, then reread it with a marking pen in hand. Underline words and phrases that seem peculiar to the subject matter. Underline other words and phrases that delight you for whatever reason—lively, witty, imaginative words that add energy and color to the subject matter.

3. *Give top priority to clarity, simplicity, concision.* For some strange reason, many beginning writers think they need to be as convoluted as possible in conveying ideas, as if simple language implies lack of sophistication. But nobody is impressed when language is used to obscure and overcomplicate rather than clarify. Consider the following passage:

> It has become quite obvious to me that the circumstances surrounding the influx of undomiciled individuals are becoming increasingly more egregious and that certain preventative measures have got to be exercised as expeditiously as feasible before the situation becomes utterly unwieldy.

Okay, this is an exaggeration, but it's not too far off; we've all met individuals whose explanations are more confusing than whatever it is they're trying to explain. Convoluted writing or speaking defeats the very purpose of communication. Let's see how we can translate the above gobbledygook into clear English:

> Because the number of homeless people is rapidly increasing, we must address the problem before it becomes unmanageable.

Eighteen words instead of forty-one—nearly two-and-a-half times shorter than the original—and the point is made much more clearly and forcefully.

But wordiness can also be caused by overreliance on flabby words, like expletives (there is, there are, etc.), as in "there are several meetings we need to have" instead of "we need to *meet* several times," or "we need to *schedule* several meetings"); auxiliary verbs (e.g., forms of the verb "to be" or "to have"); or just plain listless verbs (*went* down the slope instead of *tumbled* down the slope).

Wordiness is a writer's occupational hazard. It's almost universal that first drafts are filled with unnecessary words and phrases, which is only natural. The trick is being able to spot them during revision. Here are some common culprits that you'll want to weed out:

- *Unnecessary intensifiers* (sometimes referred to as "whoopee words," as in the following sentences:

    —That photograph was *very* shocking. "Shocking" already has the very-ness built into it; simply say "That photograph was shocking"—or better yet, "That photograph shocked me," using a strong verb instead of a weak auxiliary.

    —I was *definitely* excited by the news that I passed the test. Since no one would ever say, "I was *probably* excited ..." the definiteness of the assertion is implicit.

- *Unnecessary negation.* Whenever possible, try phrasing things in the positive. Instead of "Because we didn't have a map, we weren't able to locate the mountain lake," write "Because we lacked a map, we failed to locate the mountain lake." Using positive phrasing enables you to choose stronger verbs ("lacked" instead of "didn't have"; "failed" instead of "weren't able"), which in turn adds a greater element of conviction to your voice.

- *Inappropriate use of passive voice.* Teachers sometimes instruct their students to avoid passive-voice constructions, but this is a mistake; the passive voice serves an important function. Inappropriate use of passive voice is another matter. Now, before we proceed, let's make sure you know the difference between passive voice and active voice. *With active voice it is clear who is doing what to whom:*

Sally whacked Wally over the head with a banana.

Turned into a passive-voice construction, the sentence would read:

Wally was whacked over the head with a banana.

Here, the person doing the whacking cannot be determined; we only know that the grammatical subject (Wally) is being acted upon. But that does not *necessarily* mean it's a weaker sentence. If the author did not want anyone to know that it was Sally who whacked Wally (perhaps because it happened in the dark), then the passive construction would be appropriate. When you were a kid, you might have used passive voice to report an accident without directly admitting that you were the perpetrator, as in the sentence, "Mom, the living room window just got broken!"

How would you react if you were to read in tomorrow's headlines, "WAR HAS BEEN DECLARED"? Most likely by wondering "*Who* is declaring war on *whom*?" In such a context, active voice is necessary. Similarly, when you're writing up an experiment for a lab report, it would be a mistake to use anything but passive voice in describing your procedures. "Next, sulfuric acid was added to the solution," not "Next, Margaret and I added sulfuric acid to the solution." *Who* adds the sulfuric acid is irrelevant in the context of a lab report.

Passive constructions are also inappropriate when the writer wants to make a direct, confident assertion. Rather than, "The national record for the 50-meter dash was broken by me," it would be better to write, "I broke the national record for the 50-meter dash."

• *Redundant expressions* "Redundant" means more than is necessary. In mechanical or electrical devices, redundancy is a good thing because if one system fails to function, a backup (or redundant) system will kick in. Thus, if a hospital experiences a power outage, a redundant system such as a backup generator will immediately kick in to keep respirators or heart-lung machines working. But when it comes to writing, redundancy—using more words than are necessary—can interfere with readability and make your prose seem flaccid. In the sentence "In my opinion, I think we should eat more vegetables," the first five words are redundant because it is obvious that the speaker is expressing an opinion (the word "should" is a giveaway).

Biased and Inclusive Usage: a Commonsensical Approach

Words like *policeman, mailman, stewardess*; phrases like "best man for the job" or "lady doctor" are considered to be biased usage today. Once upon

Redundant Expressions and Revisions

Instead of ...	Write instead ...	Because ...
He began to experience dizziness.	Dizziness overcame him.	Dizziness implicitly is something that's experienced.
I stopped smoking in light of the fact that it became difficult to breathe.	I stopped smoking because it became difficult to breathe.	One word, "because," does the job of six ("in light of the fact that").
Silk is a fabric that I love to wear.	I love wearing silk.	Not necessary to explain that silk is a fabric.
My eyes watched the stranger.	I watched the stranger.	What else do you watch things with?
The music caused a soothing feeling inside of Gloria.	The music soothed Gloria.	"Soothing" is a feeling; turning "a soothing feeling" into a verb ("soothed") condenses the sentence, as well as strengthens it with a more precise verb.
Gloria is a person who enjoys painting.	Gloria enjoys painting.	Not necessary to point out that Gloria is a person.
Gerald's teaching methods are somewhat unique.	Gerald's teaching methods are unique.	Unique means "nothing else like it"and would not logically take a modifier.

a time, only men were hired for law enforcement or for delivering the mail, and only women were hired to tend to passengers' needs aboard airplanes, but that is no longer the case. Hence, *police officer, mail carrier,* and *flight attendant* are the more acceptable terms.

Some words, though, like *freshman, mankind,* or *manned* are not as easy to get rid of. Should we say *freshperson*? That sounds comical. *First-year student*? This may be better (many of my colleagues use this expression), but it requires four syllables instead of two. Launch a *staffed* spacecraft? Doesn't quite work, does it? Common sense dictates that, in cases like these, the older usage is still best.

Avoiding Vacant and Insincere Usage

Thanks mainly to advertising, words are often used to create irrational associations, or to create an impression that they mean something more than the context provides. Context is everything, of course; words in themselves are neither sincere or insincere, meaningless or meaningful.

Let's consider a couple of examples of vacant or insincere usage. What could the word *charm* possibly mean in the sentence, "Put *charm* into your smile by brushing with Vibradent"? Advertisers do not want consumers to think about the matter at all, but only to subconsciously assume that by brushing their teeth with Vibradent toothpaste, they will automatically become *charming.*

As a writer, you want to avoid using words so disingenuously. Here are a few examples of such usage:

Your painting is *interesting.*

This sounds almost like an insult, and rightly so. Respond to someone's work in a more specific way, such as "Your color combinations create a dreamlike effect."

Paul offered *meaningful* suggestions.

The word "meaningful" is almost meaning*less;* better to specify a kind of meaningfulness, such as *practical* or *highly relevant.*

Studying literature is a *worthwhile* pursuit

Like *meaningful* and *interesting, worthwhile* is a vague, catchall word that conveys little information about the nature of the pursuit. Better to recast the sentence into something like:

"Studying literature gives one a deeper understanding
of human behavior in different social or cultural settings.

Having Fun with Words or Dancing with Figures of Speech

Figures of speech comprise the *jeu d'esprit* that lies at the heart of language. It's as old as the oldest poetry (Homer's "rosy fingers of dawn" or the "whale road" seas of the *Beowulf* poet for example). Figurative language, which includes all sorts of fancy tropes (i.e., imaginative turns of phrase) that have been given polysyllabic Greek names—metonymy, synecdoche, synesthesia*—names that can give even graduate students, *Jeopardy!* fans, and college profs, like yours truly, a headache, but the point I want to stress here is that figurative language delights readers.

Figurative language is usually associated with poetry, but you find it in fiction and essay writing everywhere, even in science writing. Here's an especially fine example by K.C. Cole from a section of her book, *The Hole in the Universe*, in which she writes about the history of numbers:

The Western world really didn't play much of a role in zero's career until a young Italian named Leonardo Pisano, schooled by Muslim teachers in the Hindu Arabic number system, took it upon himself to bring these new num-

---

* Did I pique your curiosity? Very well: *metonymy* is a kind of symbolism whereby a concrete object represents an abstraction: "He took to the *bottle*" for "He started drinking alcoholic beverages" is a verbal form of metonymy, so commonly used that no one appreciates the fact that it's figurative language. *Synecdoche* is a part of something representing the whole: "My daughter finally got her *wheels*" (actually, she got the whole car with the wheels attached). *Synesthesia* is where one form of sensory image invokes an image belonging to another sense: "The rain *felt gray*"; "I could *smell the sweetness* of the wine." Want more? A good place to start is *Figures of Speech: 60 Ways to Turn a Phrase* by Arthur Quinn (Salt Lake City: Gibbs-Smith, 1982).

bers to the West—still mired at the time in clunky Roman numerals. Those ponderous Xs and Ms and Ls were impossible to put to use for calculation; one could only line them up like so many classical pillars, set in concrete (or marble, as the case may be). They had no sense of place; an X at the beginning of a sequence could mean almost the same as an X at the end; the only way to add was to pile on more letters, or invent new ones. Roman numerals were about as useful for math as hood ornaments. They could only make a statement, not take you for a ride.

> K. C. Cole, *The Hole in the Universe: How Scientists Peered Over the Edge of Emptiness and Found Everything*. NY: Harcourt, 2001.

Just as Cole humanizes the history of numbers by calling attention to Leonardo Pisano (the early thirteenth-century mathematician who became more famously known by his nickname Fibonacci), so does she give character to numbers themselves—in this case Roman numerals—by using metaphorical language to describe their inability to function in calculation: "They had no sense of place"; they were "as useful for math as hood ornaments." (Yes, comparisons using "like" or "as" technically are *similes*, but similes are simply a more explicit form of metaphorical language.) Metaphor, in other words, can facilitate comprehension as it delights.

A Closer Look at Metaphor

Just as human nature lies at the heart of any subject, so too does it lie at the heart of language itself. Metaphorical language is language that embodies abstractions with concrete images (e.g., *brick wall* to represent opacity). One of my favorite metaphors is the one that Christopher Morley used to describe New York City:

New York is the nation's thyroid gland.

Now, if Morley had written, "New York is characterized by hyperactivity," the impact would not be nearly as keen.

One of the masters of metaphorical language is Martin Luther King, Jr., as this passage from his famous "I Have a Dream" speech indicates:

> America has given the Negro people a bad check: a
> check which has come back marked "insufficient funds."
> But we refuse to believe that the bank of justice is bankrupt.

When you are addressing an abstraction such as racial injustice— especially to a large audience (King had addressed a quarter of a million people who had filled the Mall in Washington, DC on that August day in 1963), you will want to use words that convey abstractions instantly, which is what metaphors or linked metaphors, like "bad check" ... "insufficient funds" ... "bank of justice," achieve. In this way, too, the abstractions are *humanized*—that is, brought into the arena of everyday human activity.

People Words

There is another kind of figurative language that I like to think of as "people words"—words that literally represent the actions or achievements of individuals. Have you ever been called *quixotic*? Have your speeches been described as *mesmerizing*? Did you ever overhear complaints about workloads being *herculean*, even *sisyphean*? What did your boss mean when she referred to one of your coworkers, the one who dislikes computers, as a *luddite*? These are just a few of the many words that originated as names of individuals—real, fictional, or mythological. People words call attention to the fact that the human dimension fascinates even at the level of word choice.

By the way, in case you're not familiar with the above words…

> • *quixotic*, from Don Quixote, the hero of Cervantes'
> novel by that name: an impractical romantic adven-
> turer.
>
> • *mesmerize*, from Friedrich Mesmer, 1735–1815, an
> early psychologist who first experimented with what
> became hypnosis, known then as mesmerism, now
> meaning to captivate or keep enthralled.

- *herculean*, from Hercules, the strong man from Greek mythology who had to perform twelve incredibly difficult labors to win immortality; now meaning any unusually difficult task.

- *sisyphean*, from Sisyphus, the poor chump from Greek mythology condemned to roll a rock up a hill, only to have it roll back down, so he can roll it back up … and so on through eternity. Today it refers to an exercise in futility.

- *luddite*, one who hates machines—or all of technology. From Ned Ludd, an eighteenth-century laborer at the dawn of the Industrial Revolution in England, who led a group of angry coworkers to smash up the machinery that was threatening their jobs.

Getting Curious about Word Origins

Learning common prefixes, suffixes, and roots can help you increase your ability to determine the meanings of unfamiliar words. And, because words are like miniature history books, their embedded ancient meanings can enhance the human dimension of your writing as well as shed light on the history of a period. For example, knowing the origins of the names for days of the week or months reminds us of a time when Norse, Greek, or Roman gods were a pervasive presence in everyday life.

EXERCISES

1. Learn about the person—real, fictitious, or mythological—behind the following words or expressions (as well as learn the word or expression if you don't know it already):

    (a) machiavellian

    (b) protean

    (c) procrustean bed

    (d) dunce

    (e) sadist

Prefixes, Roots, and Suffixes
Worth Learning

PREFIXES

Prefixes Relating to Number

ONE	mono- [monocle; monopoly]; uni- [unicorn; united]
TWO	du- [duet]; di- [divide]; bi- [binary]
THREE	tri- [triangle]
FOUR	quadr- [quadrangle]; tetr- [tetralogy]
FIVE	penta- [pentagon]; quin- [quintuplets]
SIX	sex- [sextet]; hexa- [hexagram]
SEVEN	sept- [septet; September*]
	hepta- [heptameter (verse line with seven beats)]
EIGHT	oct- [octagon; October*]
NINE	non- [nonagenarian]; nov- [novena; November*]
TEN	deca- [decathlon]; decim- [decimal; December*]

* In ancient times, September, October, November, and December were the seventh, eighth, ninth, and tenth months of the year, respectively]

Prefixes Relating to Time

BEFORE; FIRST	ante- [anteroom]; fore- [forenoon]; pre- [previous]
AFTER	post- [postpone]
AGAIN	re- [review]
AT THE SAME TIME	syn- [synchronize]

Prefixes Relating to Direction or Orientation

ABOVE	super- [supersede]; hyper- [hyperactive]
ACROSS	trans- [transcontinental]
AGAINST	anti- [antidote]; contra- [contrary]
AROUND	circum- [circumnavigate]
BELOW	sub- [submarine]; hypo- [hypothermia]
BOTH; EITHER WAY	ambi- [ambidextrous, ambivalent]
BACKWARD	re- [reverse]; retro- [retroactive]
BETWEEN	inter- [interview]
FORWARD	pro- [propel]
OUTSIDE OF	e- [eject]; ec- [eccentric]; ex- [external]
TOGETHER	en- [ensemble]; sym- [symphony]
WITHIN	intra- [intradepartmental]

	Prefixes Relating to Positives or Negatives
BAD	dis- [disaster*]; mal- [malicious]
GOOD	eu- [euphonic]
NOT	a- [asymptomatic]; non- [nonentity]; un- [unappetizing]; il- [illegitimate]; in- [invisible]

* Meaning literally *bad star*, revealing the astrological origin of this word.

SUFFIXES

	Adjectival Suffixes
CAPABLE OF BEING	-able [enjoyable]; -ible [pliable]
SHOWING CHAR-ACTERISTICS OF	-ful [wonderful]; -ic [psychic] -ical [diabolical]; -ous [famous]; -y [fussy]
LACKING	-less [hopeless]

	Noun Suffixes
BELIEF, IDEOLOGY	-ism [Hinduism; Marxism]
ONE WHO	-ist [Marxist; individualist] -ant [celebrant]; -ent [dissident] -er [carpenter]
STATE OF BEING	-ness [happiness] -tion [inspiration]

	Verbal Suffixes
	-ate, -en, -ify, and -ize. [All verbal suffixes mean "cause to happen": implicate; frighten; magnify; recognize]

ROOTS

BOOK	biblios [Bible, bibliography]
CARRY	fer [ferry]; port [portable]
EARTH	geo, ter [geothermal, terrestrial]
EMPTY	vac [vacuum]
WRITE	graph, scrib, scrip [telegraph, scribble, script]
HAND	manu [manuscript, manufacture]
ALL	omni [omniscient]
FEELING, EMOTION	path, passio [sympathy, impassioned]
MIND, SOUL	psych [psychology; psyche]
SPEECH, WORD	dict, log, loqui [dictionary; logic; loquacious; eloquent]
FAR	tele [televise]
MAN	vir [virile]

2. Define the italicized prefix, suffix and/or root in the following words. How does its meaning relate to the modern definition of the whole word? Use the dictionary if you need help.

(a) mono*logue*

(b) *decimate*

(c) *va*cation

(d) *sub*sid*ize*

(e) de*ify*

(f) *teleportation*

(f) a*chromatic*

(g) *geo*de

(h) *vir*tue

3. Create one or more sentences in which you use the following words metaphorically. Example: plow

Harriet plowed into her backlog of paperwork.

Our training program was the plow that cultivated a new field of job opportunities.

(a) scalpel

(b) plate

(c) coin (or a particular type of coin)

(d) lantern

(e) basement

Part
Five

Shepherding Your Lifewriting
Essays into Print or Cyberspace

15

Selling Your Lifewriting to Newspapers, Literary Journals, and Magazines

In this Chapter
~ Knowing your market
~ Writing a query letter
~ The newspaper market
~ The literary journal market
~ The commercial magazine market
~ The e-zine market

If you have worked your way up to this chapter and didn't turn here first, then congratulations; it is tempting to market one's work prematurely. And, even after you have perfected your craft, editors will not pay much attention to you unless you follow standard professional practices of literary marketing.

Welcome to the business side of publishing, where editors are forever searching out talented writers who can fulfill their publishing agendas. There is never a shortage of writers, mind you, not even of talented writers. But what of writers who can provide the material editors need to keep their publications financially healthy and reputable? Those numbers are never large.

In this chapter you will learn the steps necessary for selling your lifewriting features; in the next chapter you will learn how to sell a book project.

Knowing Your Market

One of the most common mistakes beginning writers make is to submit their work indiscriminately to whatever magazine or book publisher comes to mind. Doing so wastes your time and the editor's time. It is also an easy way to become quickly discouraged, unless one has a fondness for collecting rejection slips. One of the best pieces of advice I can give you when it comes to selling your writing is to become thoroughly acquainted with the publisher or publication you're considering sending your work to. This does not mean simply to read the editorial requirements in *Writer's Market* or scan a table of contents. *Rather, it includes the following*:

1. Study the periodical's writer's guidelines. Editors prepare guidelines describing exactly what they are looking for from freelancers. Find them in *The American Directory of Writer's Guidelines*, on the Internet, or send a self-addressed, stamped envelope to the publisher with a note requesting a copy of its writer's guidelines.

2. Get an overall feel for a magazine you are thinking of submitting to —gauge its personality, how it differs from other periodicals. Think of periodicals like *The Atlantic Monthly, Cosmopolitan, Family Circle, The New Yorker, Rolling Stone, Wired*—each has a distinct appearance and format. Each has its own personality, if you will, consistently publishing a distinctive type of writing and aiming for a distinctive readership—customers who come to expect the same kind of material in the same style, voice, and length.

3. Read *all* of the features in a single issue of the periodical. Do the same with three or four back issues. In a notebook, keep a record of recurring characteristics. This takes time, of course, but it is time well spent. You will gain insight into the kinds of

material the editorial staff likes to publish. At the same time, you will internalize the recurring techniques of professional writers—tone of voice, organizational schemes, use of examples, ways of opening and concluding effectively.

4. Learn the characteristics of the periodical's target audience: Is the periodical mainly intended for young homemakers? Urbane intellectuals? Blue collar workers? Athletes? Outdoors people? How is the target audience reflected in the subject matter of the articles published? In the level of formality? In the advertisements?

5. Pay attention to the length of the features in a given issue. Do the lengths vary? Are they consistently long or short? If a magazine regularly uses features that are four thousand words long, don't offer them a manuscript that's two thousand or eight thousand words long. By the way, always include the word count in the upper right hand corner of the first page of your manuscript.

Writing a Query Letter

The query letter is an essential tool for a writer of nonfiction to master. Rather than submit the manuscript cold, query the editor first. In the case of newspapers and small-circulation (under 20,000) commercial magazines, consider including the manuscript with the query letter *if* the feature is truly finished. That will give you a competitive edge in case you've aroused the editor's curiosity with your letter. Many of the high-circulation commercial magazines, however, prefer receiving a query letter separately. When submitting to literary journals, submit just the manuscript unless the editorial guidelines direct otherwise.

Give your query letter the same kind of attention you give to your feature. After all, that letter will constitute the first sampling of your writing, and it pays to make a strong first impression. The following guidelines will help you write the kind of letter an editor would have a hard time saying "no" to:

1. Address the letter to an editor by name—not to "The Editor" or "Nonfiction Editor" or "Editorial Dept."—unless you are

specifically instructed to do so. Usually, the appropriate editor's name is given in the market listing, or inside the periodical itself—but if you cannot find it, look for a telephone number and call the periodical.

2. Summarize your feature idea in a strong, concise language. Even a particularly appealing topic will not pass muster if you do not present it engagingly.

Let's say you've written a profile of your amateur-astronomer neighbor, the one we talked about in Chapter 3, and you're ready to pitch the feature. Avoid verbose, clunky sentences such as "I'm in the process of writing a profile of my neighbor, who involves her whole family in the joys and challenges of amateur astronomy." Half the words in that sentence are useless. The fact that you are in the process of writing a profile is obvious. "Joys and challenges" sounds like trite advertising copy. Instead, present a condensed version of the profile itself. See query letter (b) in the sidebar below.

3. Refrain from being superficially clever or telling the editor how terrific you think your piece is or how urgently your ideas need to get into print. Such remarks will brand you as a rank amateur.

4. Say a few things about your qualifications for writing the piece. Don't include your entire resume.

5. Always include a stamped, self-addressed envelope (SASE), and make sure it's large enough and has the proper amount of postage affixed (not paper clipped) to it. Publishers would quickly go bust if they had to pay return postage on the hundreds of unsolicited manuscripts they receive each month. If you do not want the manuscript returned, then say so in your letter, and include a #10 (business-sized), stamped, self-addressed envelope instead. Keep in mind, however, that editors occasionally write comments on the manuscript if it was a near hit. If you include only a #10 envelope, you'll miss out on these comments.

6. Do not submit e-queries unless the periodical specifically requests them. While the number of editors preferring e-queries and even e-submissions is increasing—a few editors even *require*

freelancers to submit their work electronically—most editors prefer to receive queries by snail mail. Always read over an editor's submission guidelines carefully.

7. Include photocopies of any articles you've published, especially if you can tie them to the article you're querying about. Editors want to know just how professional a writer you are or are trying to become.

8. It is perfectly all right to query an editor about an unfinished piece, provided you're confident about its contents and can provide at least an approximate date for its completion. With books, writers typically include a query letter with a detailed proposal (discussed in Chapter 16).

9. Look for the editor's policy on simultaneous submissions. Most editors are willing to read a manuscript that is being considered elsewhere, but they prefer to know that up front. And of course, if a simultaneous-submission manuscript is accepted, you must inform the other editors of that fact.

10. For seasonal features, editors of monthly and even weekly magazines require several months' lead time. If you wish to propose a Christmas feature, say, then query the editor (and have your feature at least well underway) no later than May or June. Newspaper editors do not need that much lead time: Query them about seasonal material three months ahead of time.

The Newspaper Market

Even though the ratio of freelance to staff-written newspaper features is slender (and varies in degree from newspaper to newspaper) most newspapers are published daily or weekly, which requires a lot of material and makes them a promising market for beginners. Newspapers don't pay well for freelance material, but your audience generally is large. Your local newspaper is likely to be receptive to locally-written freelance features, even from beginning writers, so start with them.

Because the competition to be published is stiffer in major metro newspapers like *The Boston Globe*, the *New York Times* and *The Chicago Tribune*, you may want to focus on smaller newspapers first.

Sample Query Letters (with Commentary)

(a) Letter describing a feature for a newspaper:

[date]
Henrietta Winsom, Features Editor
Waco Gazette
Waco, Texas

Dear Ms. Winsom:

As a reading tutor for children who are non-native speakers of English I have been successful in raising my pupils' English-reading proficiency in a relatively short time through the use of various games. Not just games like *Jeopardy!* and *Trivia Pursuit*, but role-playing games. For example, I put the children in the role of tutor, and they must come up with strategies (in English!) to help *me* learn words and phrases in their native language. Being a Waco resident, I assume that readers of your newspaper would be interested in how my E.S.L. teaching methods are helping young non-native children in our community enhance their literacy skills.

A draft of the feature is enclosed, together with an SASE. I look forward to hearing from you.

Sincerely yours,
Selena Smith

Selena Smith's letter is crisply, concisely written. No query letter should exceed one page. It is upbeat in tone, but not excessively so. Selena alludes to her credentials, but only as they relate to the subject-matter of the feature. Selena gives just enough specific information about her tutoring achievement to make the editor want to read the feature. Notice, too, how she calls attention to her being a local resident. Newspaper editors like to champion local writers.

(b). Letter describing a profile for a magazine:

[date]
Ingrid Starr, Managing Editor
Amateur Astronomer Magazine
Tombstone, Arizona

Dear Ms. Starr:

Can amateur astronomy improve family togetherness and psychological well-being? My amateur-astronomer neighbor proved that it can, and in several fascinating ways. After interviewing her and doing research on her telescopic equipment, astronomy clubs, local observatories, and other resources available to amateur astronomers, I have written a feature that focuses not only on the recreational dimension of "backyard" astronomy (there are, as you know, numerous features on that topic), but on the particular ways in which this hobby brings family members together. For example, my neighbor's 10-year-old daughter learned to identify—and *track,* using an 8" Celestron—several lesser-known constellations, as well as star clusters, galaxies, and nebulae. She then proceeded to teach her astonished parents to use the instrument properly, giving a whole new (and healthy) meaning to the term "parental guidance."

I call attention to other family-related interactions as well: each family member is responsible for a particular sky search or a particular use of one of the telescopes or a particular area of astronomy; visits to observatories, trips with other astronomers, and so on.

My article is finished and ready to be submitted. It is not under consideration elsewhere. Please let me know if you are interested in seeing it. A #10 SASE is enclosed for your reply.

Sincerely yours,
Jane Fuller

Continued on next page

Instead of opening with a humdrum sentence like "I have just finished writing a feature about how amateur astronomy can serve as an ideal hobby for the entire family," the writer conveys the gist of the feature itself, posing the premise as a question to pique curiosity: "Can amateur astronomy improve family togetherness and psychological well being?" Notice how, in highlighting salient points, she seamlessly alludes to the research (both primary and secondary) she has conducted in preparation for writing the piece, and demonstrates her expertise by alluding to technical details about the telescope. Note too, that she assures the editor that the piece is not being considered for publication elsewhere. Although many editors these days accept simultaneous submissions, some do not.

As with magazines, familiarize yourself with the newspaper you're considering submitting to. Read the features similar to your own, then visit the paper's Web site for contact information. For a full listing of newspapers published in the U.S., consult the *Gale Directory of Publications and Broadcast Media* (published annually) at your public library.

Kinds of Lifewriting Features Newspapers Like

Along with insightful commentary on current events, newspaper editors like to publish lively human-interest features to balance out the straight news. Such features can include current fads ("hot topics"), practical, time- or money-saving ideas, travel tips, and book reviews. Many of these topics are covered by staff writers or syndicated columnists, but editors occasionally like to bring in fresh voices from the community.

Length is important. Newspapers seldom publish freelance features over 750 words, and most features run between 500 and 650 words.

Usually you should address your query letter and/or submission either to the features editor or to the editorial page editor. Be sure to find the name of the appropriate editor; don't simply address your submission to an editor generically. Be sure to enclose a stamped, self-addressed envelope.

The Literary Journal Market

Aside from your local newspaper, the likeliest place to find your way into print is through the literary journal market. Although the competition is rigorous—only about one to three percent of material submitted gets accepted—the market is large, and the editorial tastes are as eclectic as you can imagine. Truly, this is a market to study carefully.

Literary Journals: An Overview

The term "literary journal" (or the less flattering "little magazine") refers to those mostly small-circulation, not-for-profit publications, often sponsored by universities or writers' organizations, which appear between one and twelve times a year. Because they are not dependent on commercial sponsors, they tend not to cater to mass appeal. They are more willing to publish innovative work that takes more controversial or offbeat stances than "mainstream" material. Also, although the competition for breaking into reputable literary journals is almost as tough as breaking into mass-circulation magazines, literary-journal editors usually are more receptive to new writers.

While many literary journals these days emphasize fiction and/or poetry, with maybe a personal essay or two included per issue, several journals feature essays of all kinds: personal interactions with the natural world, in-depth studies of individuals involved in social reform, victims of injustice, up-close-and-personal looks at unusual people doing unusual work. The International Directory of Little Magazines and Small Presses (Dustbooks) lists over 6,000 places you can sell your writing, so your opportunities abound.

You can often find a journal you think might be interested in your work at your local public library or in one of the larger bookstore chains. If you can't find it there, purchase a sample copy from the journal itself so you can familiarize yourself with its contents.

Some journals devote parts of their issues—sometimes entire issues—to a single theme. For example, The Sun Magazine, one of the few literary journals with a large circulation (50,000), has recently invited its readers to submit essays on topics such as "Whirlwind Romances," "Locked Doors," "Begging," and "Fathers and Sons." (Simply hearing those topic designations can get a lifewriter's mind spinning with ideas of his or her own!)

Besides *The International Directory of Little Magazines and Small Presses*, check the latest edition of *The American Directory of Writer's Guidelines*, *The Writer's Handbook*, *Writer's Market*, or *Writer's Yearbook* for journals that are receptive to lifewriting essays.

Essay Competitions

Some literary journals sponsor annual or bi-annual essay competitions, so be sure to check for guidelines about those. *Writer's Market*, each issue of *Writer's Digest*, *The Writer*, and *Poets & Writers Magazine* publish announcements for many of these competitions. Here is a sampling of these contests (note that all require entry fees):

The $4,000 Narrative Prize. Annual award given to a work of literary nonfiction published in *Narrative Magazine*. See the guidelines at <www.narrativemagazine.com>

Annie Dillard Award for Nonfiction. Annual prize sponsored by *Bellingham Review*. See the guidelines at <www.ac.wwu.edu/~bhreview>

The Lamar York Prize for Nonfiction. $1,000 and publication in *Chattahoochee Review*. Deadline: January 31 of each year. See guidelines at <www.chattahoochee-review.org>

Literal Latté Ames Essay Award. Deadline: September 15 each year. Write to *Literal Latté*, 61 East Eighth St., Suite 240, New York, NY 10003. <www.literal-latte.com>

Missouri Review Editor's Prize for the Essay. $2,000 and publication in *Missouri Review*. Deadline: October 15 each year. Write to *Missouri Review*, 1507 Hillcrest Hall, University of Missouri, Columbia, Columbia, MO 65211. <www.missourireview.com>

New Letters Dorothy Churchill Capon Creative Nonfiction Prize. Deadline: May 20 of each year. Write to *New Letters*, 5101 Rockhill Rd., Rm. 222, University of Missouri, Kansas City MO 64110. <www.umkc.edu/newletters>

New Millennium Writings Award for Nonfiction. Deadlines vary. Write to *New Millennium Writings*, P. O. Box 2463, Knoxville, KY 37901. <www.mach2.com>

The Commercial Magazine Market

Being published in a popular magazine with a circulation in the hundreds of thousands or even in the millions is nearly every writer's dream—not just because these magazines pay well, but because they can quickly build a writer's reputation and are great for the ego. True, "big name" writers often are invited to submit features to such magazines, but it is also true that unknowns occasionally are plucked from the slush piles.

Is the competition fierce? A better word might be *ferocious*. Out of every two hundred submissions, one or two might make the cut (the odds are better with the regional magazines). But as one of my professors said to me years ago, there's always room at the top. If you work hard on making your writing the best it can possibly be—I mean work *relentlessly* hard on your writing, there's no reason to doubt your highest aspirations. But give yourself plenty of time to master your craft, master your subject matter, and never give up.

Lifewriting that Makes the Grade in Commercial Magazines

Turn to a recent issue of a magazine you dream of getting published in and thoroughly study the lifewriting features in it. As I write this I'm paging through the September/October 2003 issue of *Mother Jones*—a magazine with a circulation of close to 200,000 that focuses on progressive issues in popular culture—it is published by the Foundation for National Progress, headquartered in San Francisco. Here is a lovely photo-essay about great blues artists Honeyboy Edwards, B.B. King, W.C. Handy, Bessie Smith, and others by veteran music writer David Hajdu—the occasion being that 2003 had been designated "the year of the blues." Here is a profile of New York gynecologist William Rashbaum, M.D., one of the oldest living late-term abortion doctors. The feature, by Rebecca Paley, a reporter and staff correspondent for *People* Magazine, presents a vivid, in-depth look at this controversial doctor and his patients (among them, a 14–year old rape victim). And here is a profile, by the essayist Ian Frazier, of the British eighteenth-century general Henry Shrapnel who invented—you guessed it, the exploding cannonball.

What these superb examples of lifewriting have in common are the following:

- vivid, forceful writing
- in depth research
- richly textured reportage—by which I mean the information builds toward a larger understanding of the social or historical circumstances in question
- the people are brought into sharp focus, much the way novelists bring their characters into focus: with detailed descriptions of physical and behavioral characteristics

A Survey of the Commercial Magazine Market

There are six main categories of commercial magazines: Topical, Intellectual, Ideological/ Religious, Inflight, Juvenile/Teen, and Regional.

Topical magazines are subject-specific. Name a subject and there are most likely magazines devoted to it: animals and pets, nature and the outdoors, sports (or a particular sport), travel, home and garden, hobbies of one kind or another, the sciences and technology (or a particular science or technology), and the arts. Examples: *Cat Fancy, Outdoor Life, Golf Digest, Better Homes & Gardens, Crafts Magazine, Astronomy, Art & Antiques.*

Intellectual magazines aim for college-educated professionals seeking in-depth analysis of national and global issues, academic subjects, and culture. Examples include *American History, The New Yorker, The New York Review of Books, The Atlantic Monthly, Smithsonian.*

Ideological or religious magazines are oriented to a particular religious denomination or political or cultural perspective. Several of these magazines are slanted to juvenile or young-adult audiences. Examples include *Christianity Today, Evangel, Free Inquiry, Guide: True Stories Pointing to Jesus* (10–14 years), *The Lutheran Digest, U.S. Catholic.*

Inflight magazines generally focus on business, profiles of extraordinary people, high-tech innovations, contemporary lifestyles, sports, and travel. Examples include *Hemispheres* (United Airlines) and *Southwest Airlines Spirit.* Some inflight magazines are regional in character, such as *Meridian* (Midway Airlines), which favors topics relating to East Coast destinations.

Juvenile/Teen/Young Adult magazines publish features on issues that concern young people relevant to their age group, gender, and ethnicity. *Chickadee Magazine,* for example, includes personal-experience and crafts-related features for children between ages six and nine. *Girl's Life*, intended for girls between ages nine and fifteen, publishes thematic issues such as back to school, Valentine's Day, relationships with boys, Mother's Day, and Father's Day. Many magazines for young people are oriented to a particular religious faith.

Regional magazines publish features tied to a particular metropolitan area, state, or geographical region. Examples include *Gulfshore Life*, which focuses on the history, lifestyle and culture of southwest Florida (Venice, Port Charlotte, Ft. Myers, Naples, etc.); *Alabama Heritage*, published by the University of Alabama, which focuses on the history and culture of the state, whereas *Alabama Living*, published by the Alabama Rural Electric Association, focuses on outdoor, gardening, and nostalgia pieces as well as Alabama history; *Yankee*, published in New Hampshire, publishes essays about people and culture in New England.

The E-Zine Market

Although thousands of online magazines ("e-zines") exist, a significant prestige gap still exists between print magazines and their electronic counterparts.

Writers, including yours truly, are drawn to e-zines. The competition hasn't been quite as fierce on the most part, but this appears to be rapidly changing. Even so, e-zines are an excellent prospect for new writers, and I strongly recommend submitting to them. The first step, of course, is to visit their Web sites to get a feel for their personalities and editorial preferences. Use the links to their mission statements, submission guidelines; read selections from current issues. Browse their archives. E-zine archives are especially noteworthy. Whatever gets published in these 'zines remains accessible for as long as the magazine exists.

Some of the most visible and, yes, prestigious, e-zines that publish lifewriting features include the *Drexel Online Journal* (published by Drexel University) at <www.drexel.edu/doj>; *The Pedestal* <thepedestalmagazine.com>; *nidus* (published by the University of Pittsburgh), <www.pitt.edu/~nidus>; and *Salon.com*. Keep in mind, too, that many print periodicals have been launching online versions of themselves, often with content that is not included in their print versions.

EXERCISES

1. Visit your local or college library and examine several issues of periodicals described in this chapter. Also, visit a few e-zines online. After reading several of the essays in these periodicals, begin outlining an essay of your own that might be suitable and interesting to one of them. When you return home, begin drafting the essay.

2. Write a query letter pitching the article idea you have outlined in Exercise 1, above.

3. Before you recycle one of your local newspapers, go through it page by page and clip articles on topics you could imagine yourself writing. Tape them into your Daybook (leave plenty of room for marginal notations) and then do the following:

(a) Reread the piece carefully.

(b) Describe in the margins what the author does to hook the reader's attention.

(c) Respond to words and sentences that delight or annoy you. Make appropriate comments in the margins.

(d) Comment on the author's use of illustrations and explanations in support of his or her general assertions. Are they effective? Why?

(e) Comment on the conclusion. Is it effective? If so, how? If not, what would make it so?

(f) Write a similar piece, using your own distinct point of view and choice of illustrations and explanations.

4. Select a commercial magazine of your choice and write a profile of its intended readership, based on the range of topics, the writing style, formatting, ads.

5. Consult one of the market guides for a magazine you've become familiar with. Study the submission guidelines carefully, and if you think there's a match, write a query letter to the editor describing your essay. Follow the query-letter guidelines in this chapter.

16

"I Could Write a Book": Here's How

In this Chapter
~ Book-length lifewriting
~ A word about memoirs
~ Structuring the book
~ Working up a book proposal
~ The cover letter
~ Some basic advice about agents
~ The lifewriting book market

Most aspiring writers dream of publishing a book, which makes wonderfully good sense, because a successful book can be both financially and professionally rewarding, and establish one's career as an author. Up until now, we've been focusing on short features, which offer new writers the best chance of learning their craft and breaking into print. If you have been diligently studying the last fifteen chapters, writing regularly in your daybook, turning your lifewriting ideas into outlines, outlines into treatments, treatments into drafts, drafts into finished essays—and have sent one or two of your labors out to market and perhaps even getting something accepted (if so, congratulations!)—then it is time to think seriously about writing a book. This chapter will guide you through this process.

Book-length Lifewriting

As I have been using the term, "lifewriting" is not just "me" centered writing; it is people and how they are treated that will sustain a reader's interest, and that is relevant to any subject, even hard science. Think of any topic at all that you would like to write a book about, and what is going to sustain interest in that topic for 60,000 to 100,000 words (the common length of a book) will be the *people* involved. As I write this, James Gleick, one of the best science writers around, has just published a captivating biography of Isaac Newton. Here's how Gleick begins the first chapter:

> Isaac Newton said he had seen farther by standing on the shoulders of giants, but he did not believe it. He was born into a world of darkness, obscurity, and magic; led a strangely pure and obsessive life, lacking parents, lovers, and friends; quarreled bitterly with great men who crossed his path; veered at least once to the brink of madness; cloaked his work in secrecy; and yet discovered more of the essential core of human knowledge than anyone before or after. He was chief architect of the modern world. He answered the ancient philosophical riddles of light and motion, and he effectively discovered gravity. He showed how to predict the courses of heavenly bodies and so established our place in the cosmos. He made knowledge a thing of substance: quantitative and exact. He established principles, and they are called his laws.
>
> James Gleick, *Isaac Newton*. New York: Pantheon, 2003.

In a single paragraph, Gleick has laid the foundation for a 270-page biography. More than that, he convinces his audience of the fascination and worthiness of his subject. Of course, you don't have to settle on a subject like Newton to write a successful biography. The lives of so-called average people can be marvelously rich in experiences that a great many readers can benefit from and delight in; it is up to you, the biographer, to probe the depths of your subject. Of course, you need to gain access to more than your subject's memories. Private documents, like photographs, letters, notebooks, and other records are necessary, and in the case of famous people, newly discovered materials are of particular importance. Gleick, for example, draws upon unpublished notebooks and letters of Newton for his biography.

Your best bet, if just starting out, would be to write about someone who has been overlooked or relegated to the margins of mainstream history. Thumbing through biographical dictionaries, both general and specialized, would be a good place to start. *Here are a few examples*:

- *Current Biography*
- *Dictionary of American Biography*
- *Dictionary of National Biography* [British]
- *Notable American Women*
- *Who's Who in the Arab World*
- *Who's Who in America*
- *Who's Who in Government*

Or, if you are interested in writing about marginalized yet intriguing persons from the depths of history, consult histories from the period and check the index and bibliography for references to lesser-known figures. For example, as I was reading David McCullough's Pulitzer-prize winning biography of John Adams, I became very curious about Adams's third son, Thomas Boylston, apparently bitten by wanderlust and "who carried a copy of *Don Quixote* in his saddlebag." Aside from that delightful tidbit, there is very little of note about Thomas Boylston in the book. But it was enough to send me searching for more information. To my knowledge, no one has written a book about this man, who (as I learned through a Web site focusing on Adams family genealogy) became a trial lawyer (one of his cases was defending the owner of a local brothel) and served as secretary to his illustrious brother, John Quincy Adams, before turning to heavy drinking and dying in debt. There's stuff here for at least a biographical essay on the man. The research would be challenging, but if lifewriting is in your blood, sleuthing is part of the fun.

A Word about Memoirs

What about your own life, you may be wondering. How many times have you uttered that mantra, "What I've gone through could fill a book"? Well, what you've gone through probably could, but as you know, experience alone is not enough. You have to shape those experiences into a coherent and engaging *story*. Remember from Chapter 4 the points I made about creating dramatic immediacy and narrating along a rising curve of expectation? Well, the same principles hold true for larger structures like biographies and memoirs.

First, let's clear up some misconceptions about memoirs. No, you don't have to be a four-star general or the C.E.O. of a corrupt organization (or even an upstanding one), or have survived a close encounter with the Abominable Snowman. No, you don't have to be a celebrity or a prodigy. Nor do you have to be in your eighties before you can write your memoirs—in a moment I'll be talking about the poet and essayist Patricia Hampl, who wrote a prize-winning memoir when she was in her thirties. However, you do have to have a purpose more substantial than "Hey, look how impressive my life has been!" Your life experiences should have the potential for striking loud chords of recognition in your readers on an emotional as well as intellectual level. The experiences of others, when conveyed vividly and forcefully, vicariously become our experiences. They enlarge our understanding of the human condition and heighten our compassion for what others endure, people who are not so different from ourselves.

How does a memoir pull this off? Let's find out by taking a look at Frank McCourt's *Angela's Ashes*, one of several recent, highly acclaimed memoirs whose authors focus on that portion of life that can provide each of us with enough material to keep writing the rest of our days: childhood. (See "Recommended Reading for Lifewriting" for brief descriptions of the other recently published memoirs.)

Born in America to Irish immigrants who met and married in New York then returned to Ireland four years later, Frank McCourt begins his memoir by wondering how, when he thinks back on his childhood, he managed to survive at all. And no wonder: His childhood consisted of abject poverty and an ongoing series of misfortunes, but—and this is part of the unforgettable charm of this book—the dramatic moments are always tempered with compassion and humor. For example, when the family, penniless, was settling into Frank's grandmother's house in Limerick, both parents and Frank's three siblings faced having to sleep on a flea-ridden mattress:

> Dad pulled on his trousers and dragged the mattress off the bed and out to the street. He filled the kettle and the pot with water, stood the mattress against the wall, pounded it with a shoe, told me to keep pouring water on the ground to drown the fleas dropping there. The Limerick moon was so bright I could see bits of it shimmering in the water and I wanted to scoop up moon bits but how could I with the fleas leaping on my legs. Dad kept pounding with the shoe and I had to run back through the house to the backyard tap for more water in the kettle and the pot. Mam [Frank's mother] said, Look at you. Your shoes are drenched and you'll catch your death and your father will surely get the pneumonia without a shoe to his foot.
>
> A man on a bicycle stopped and wanted to know why Dad was beating that mattress. Mother o'God, he said, I never heard such a cure for fleas ....

Even a short passage like this captures McCourt's narrative magic. See if you can pinpoint what contributes to it before reading on.

Dramatic immediacy is one technique. It is not enough simply to say that the mattress was flea-ridden. McCourt recreates the moment, places the reader at the scene. McCourt also uses *minute detail*—first to recreate the sensation (in the paragraph preceding the two quoted above) of hundreds of fleas "leaping, jumping, fastened to our flesh ... hopping, biting," then describing how the children tore at their flesh until they bled. What I find most remarkable about the passage above is the way the narrator can still appreciate the beauty of moonlight shimmering in the water— wanting to gather up that moonlight with his hands—in the middle of helping his father rid the mattress of fleas. That, together with the amusing reaction from the man on the bicycle, provides comic relief to what would otherwise seem like an altogether depressing moment.

One other technique to call attention to is McCourt's use of dialogue to bring the people to life. Memoirists, like novelists, must bring the people to life on the page, and dialogue (together with detailed description of appearance and behavioral quirks) is an effective way to do this. McCourt's use of dialogue is unusual in that he does not use quotation marks. For me, this makes the dialogue seem more intimately a part of the narrator's memory.

Structuring the Book

Some writers wishing to write a biography or memoir assume they must cover everything in their lives, beginning at the beginning and moving forward year by year in strict chronological order.

Boring.

Frank McCourt limits his memoir from ages four through nineteen. (A sequel, 'Tis, begins where Angela's Ashes leaves off.) The late feminist, literary critic, and mystery novelist Carolyn Heilbrun (who published her popular mysteries under the name Amanda Cross) limited her memoir, The Last Gift of Time, to her experiences after turning sixty. Why? Because these years were proving to be the most active and rewarding of her life. Instead of structuring her memoir chronologically, Heilbrun opts for topical organization, which is a more flexible and creative kind of structuring. The opening chapter focuses on her desire to purchase a home just for herself to fulfill her need for solitude even though she'd been happily married for fifty years. Her next chapter is about a dog who came to live with her. And, the chapter after that is a meditation on time.

In addition to limiting her scope, Heilbrun is determined to be lively, to speak her mind, to feel good about her eccentricities and desires. In a chapter titled "On Not Wearing Dresses," she writes:

> A Smith [College] graduation I attended at age sixty-two marked the last time I wore heels. As they sank into the mud on our way to the academic procession, and my toes could be felt crunching unhappily together, I vowed to wear them no more. I gave away all my shoes with heels and turned to flats. Dresses took a good deal longer to eschew. Although I wore trousers far more often, I would creep unhappily into panty hose and properly feminine garments before giving a speech or attending a required social event.
>
> Since I had also, with maturity, that is, at about fifty-five, given up trying to stay thin, I now needed dresses that would allow for my mid-body expansion without hanging on me like a tent I had mistakenly donned instead of slept in. I turned to catalogs—a lifesaver. But I did not at first realize that the sizes were on a different scale: a 14X bore no relation to the old 14 I had been wearing; thus the first dress I ordered was immense.
>
> Carolyn G. Heilibrun, *The Last Gift of Time: Life Beyond Sixty*. New York: Ballantine Books, 1997.

Heilbrun's natural voice is charming, unpretentious, human. It matters little that the author is one of the America's most illustrious educators and mystery novelists. In the context of this memoir, she is concerned with telling her story of how she goes about enjoying life in her autumnal years.

Don't plunge into writing your memoirs prematurely. Be patient and reflect on possible organizational schemes. Think about motifs that characterized certain stages of your life, and shape your chapters around them. A motif can be an ongoing obsession or circumstance during a particular time in your life. Maybe, when you were in college, that motif was "being out on a limb" because you were a big risk-taker back then, and during the years when you first started out in your profession you went from risk-taking to "toeing the line" (or to keep our metaphors consistent, "hugging the tree").

Patricia Hampl—poet, essayist, MacArthur "Genius" Award recipient and Regents Professor of English at the University of Minnesota—structured her Houghton Mifflin Literary Fellowship Award memoir, A *Romantic Education*, according to motifs. Published in 1981 when she was still in her thirties, the title reflects her over-arching theme of superficial vs. deep romanticism. Each of the three sections of the memoir reflects a particular related motif:

> I. St. Paul: The Garden
> II. Beauty
> III. Prague: The Castle

The first section consists, unsurprisingly, of the author's childhood years in St. Paul, Minnesota—but the focus is on her Czech grandmother, her enchanting garden, and her recollections of an all but forgotten Eastern European culture. The second section is essentially a long meditation on beauty: her grandmother's; female beauty in general; beauty in relationship to her growing consciousness as a feminist, humanist, and poet; beauty as it becomes trivialized and profaned in popular culture; and then a deeper beauty: one that can forge an aesthetic and spiritual relationship with the land and with peoples of different ethnic backgrounds—peoples that, ironically, become "romanticized" in the sense of becoming mere objects of beauty, stripped of any spiritual connection.

The third section focuses on Hampl's journey, following the death of her grandmother, to the Czech Republic out of a desire to discover her ancestral homeland and to experience for herself that dimension of beauty which an America torn by war and political unrest (this was during the Vietnam war) had lost. It is in Prague, the city of Kafka, "the city of the Western mind," where she discovers, among the "broken gardens" of a country still haunted by World War II and the Holocaust, that dimension of beauty she'd been seeking.

As you can see, Hampl's idea of memoir is both typical and atypical: It is as much a meditation on culture and art and history and human nature as it is a recollection of her own growth as an artist and a woman.

Working Up a Book Proposal

Nonfiction books are usually sold to publishers on the basis of a book proposal. As you develop your book's structure (See Chapter 5), you'll automatically be structuring much of your book proposal. Since, with a book proposal, you are demonstrating to the editor what kind of writer you are, a proposal must be well written and free of typographical errors. It is a good idea, when you think you have finished writing your proposal, to let it sit for a week, then reread it—you might be surprised at how much you want to fix before sending it out.

A book proposal consists of six parts:

1. An overview
2. A market analysis
3. Your relevant credentials
4. How you will help promote the book
5. A chapter-by-chapter synopsis (like an annotated table of contents)
6. Two or three sample chapters

Let's look at each of these elements.

The Overview

This is basically a synopsis of the book. In the overview, explain the book's scope: Will you just cover your two years in the hill country of Cambodia or will you begin the book with your birth and take it through to the present day?

List the main points you will touch upon. Perhaps you'll include the fascinating conversations you overheard among your grandfather and his World War II veteran buddies and how their ideas apply to today's military. Or maybe you'll talk about the children-raising-children syndrome where girls in their early teens struggle with becoming mothers before finishing high school, a common occurrence in some U.S. societies.

Here also, talk about the voice you will use in writing the book. Will it be warm and friendly? Curmudgeonly? Academic? Will you use humor?

Also explain what your intended readers will gain from reading your book. Will they come away with a better understanding of some part of a foreign culture? Do you hope to move them to take some sort of action? Will they find satisfaction or validation in what you write? If so, how?

A Market Analysis

Publishing is a business like any other business. That means your book must be perceived not only as publishable, but marketable and profitable.

There are three parts to a market analysis:

1. A description of the competition. Describe other books in print similar to your own. Check bookseller databases such as Amazon.com, libraries, and bookstores. Buy or borrow the books you find so you can study them carefully. Explain where these titles are successful, where they fall short, and how your book will be better or different. Be careful not to denigrate these competing books, which would appear unprofessional.

2. A description of your intended readership. Whom do you envision as being most interested in reading your book? These people will comprise your *primary* audience. Who else might conceivably be interested in reading your book? This group, and those interested in buying it as a gift for people in your primary audience, will constitute your *secondary* audience.

If you're writing a book about classic-car collectors, then your primary audience will likely consist of classic-car enthusiasts: members of classic-car societies and people who restore classic cars. Secondary readers might include scale-model artists, historians of popular culture, and antique dealers.

3. A list of nontraditional outlets. Point out where sales might be garnered beyond bookstores and libraries. Will your book be a likely candidate for use as additional reading assignments in college classes? Will specialized retailers, such as garden shops or gift boutiques, want to carry it? Are there certain businesses or nonprofit organizations that might buy your book to give to their clients?

Your Background

Editors will want to know your qualifications to write this book so it's important to include a page-long profile of yourself, focusing on what is most relevant to your book project. For example, if you have professional expertise in the subject you're writing about, then describe it. A natural qualification is that you have lived the life the book is reporting.

Many people write books on subjects about which they are passionate and for which they are willing to do the necessary research. Numerous books on scientific topics have been written by journalists who are not themselves scientists. James Gleick, well known for his book on chaos theory (*Chaos: Making a New Science*) and the biography of Sir Isaac Newton, is an example. *Los Angeles Times* science columnist K. C. Cole, writes engagingly about physics and astronomy in such books as *The Universe in a Teacup* and *A Hole in the Universe*.

If you have had articles published, include photocopies of these articles with the proposal. If you've been published frequently or you have had a book or two published, then simply list your publications. Do not include works in progress, but do include works accepted for publication if they're relevant. If you have not been published, don't say so, just don't address the subject.

How You Will Help Promote the Book

Many authors are surprised to hear that they will be expected to help promote their book, but, in today's publishing world, this is the case. Outline what you will do to generate publicity for your book. Will you set up book signings? Give seminars? Find radio shows on which to do interviews? Finance a six-city book tour? Write articles and newspaper columns that mention the book?

Often it is the author's platform—a term used to describe the ways an author can assist in selling a book—that convinces an editor to publish the book. Don't overpromise, but do list things you can and will do that will help sell the book.

The Chapter-By-Chapter Synopsis

If you want to convince your editor that you indeed have a book idea worthy of publication, you must describe each chapter of the proposed book in some detail. It should also be clear how the chapters combine to form a coherent whole. Write your sample chapters first, then write synopses of these chapters. This will give you a better feel for how to go about writing the synopses for the other chapters. Each chapter synopsis should be about 100 words long. Be sure to include a synopsis of your introduction, as well as any ancillary material you plan to include, such as an appendix or bibliography.

Sample Chapters

The chapters you supply as a part of your book proposal don't have to be the first two or three in your book, but they do need to represent your best writing. You will ultimately revise these chapters many more times before your book is published, but don't even think about that, revise and polish the proposal chapters as if they were to be carved in granite.

The Cover Letter

Once you finish your proposal, you need to draft a cover letter to accompany it. Plan your letter very carefully; it is the first thing the editor will read. In one page max, describe your book: its purpose, its key features, and its organizational scheme. Describe it in a way that sparks curiosity. Think of the editor as a representative reader who is looking for indications that reading your work will be worth his or her valuable time. As with other kinds of writing, your opening paragraph has got to snag attention. Which of the following versions of a letter proposing a book on the history of ice cream would snag *your* attention?

(a) Dear Ms. Lu:

I am working on a book about the history of ice cream in the United States. Most people do not realize that this popular confection has an interesting history, even when it is stripped of all the myths. In my opinion this topic is capable of attracting a huge audience. Existing books on this fascinating topic do not include the whole story, especially of the people.

(b) Dear Ms. Lu:

Ice cream probably was not discovered by Marco Polo when he visited China in the thirteenth century; nor was it likely invented by Charles I's cook in the early seventeenth century. These and other myths have never been substantiated. And even though two books about the history of ice cream have been published (see my market analysis), there are many more stories to tell—especially about the people, such as that of a former slave who created a desert made of frozen cream and fruit after going into the catering business. The book I am proposing focuses on those all-but-forgotten individuals who shaped the earliest history of ice cream in the United States.

The second letter is the stronger of the two, for these reasons:

1. The writer launches into a conversation about the book instead of opening, as he did in version (a), with a redundant statement that he is "working on a book ...." This is made obvious when you explain what the book is about.

2. The writer demonstrates that he is knowledgeable about the topic by the details mentioned and the citing of erroneous information. In his first version, he assumed that merely alluding to the fact that myths about the history of ice cream exist is enough. It is not.

3. The writer contrasts the book to existing books: This book is centered on the people who make up the early history of ice cream.

Some Basic Advice about Agents

Glance at the market profiles of the big commercial book publishers—Random House, Harper Collins, Houghton Mifflin, Simon and Schuster, Doubleday—and what do you see? *Agented submissions only*. The reason is simple, these publishers received so many submissions, it became unprofitable to employ enough assistant editors to screen out the one percent of material worthy of serious consideration. When an agent submits a manuscript, the understanding is that the agent has already done the screening. If you have a marketable idea and a well-written proposal, then you should not have a problem finding an agent.

There are a number of guides that list contact information for literary agents, including *Literary Market Place* and *Writer's Market*. You can also find an agent by networking with other authors, attending writer's conferences, or by checking the acknowledgment page of a book similar to yours. If an agent handled a book similar to yours, he's more likely to be interested in handling your book than an agent selected at random.

Check to see if the agent you are thinking of contacting is a member of The Association of Authors' Representatives (aar-onlin.org). Member agents have agreed to adhere to a canon of ethics that relegates how they conduct their business. For one thing, an AAR member is forbidden to charge reading fees. Not all reputable agents are members of AAR, but members of AAR are likely to be reputable.

The AAR has a list of questions for you to ask an agent *after* he has offered to represent you. Reputable agents will not object to answering these questions, nor will they skirt the issue by saying they are too busy to answer them. Be wary of agents who want to charge you for anything beyond the actual photocopying and postage costs incurred in marketing your proposal to a publisher.

Make contact with an agent as you would with the editor of a book publisher. Once you have ascertained from the guides that the agent handles the type of book you are writing, send in a complete proposal, as described above. Be sure to enclose a return envelope of sufficient size, with sufficient postage attached. Some literary agents have their own Web sites and may invite inquiries by e-mail.

The Lifewriting Book Market

Editorial requirements and policies change rapidly in the book publishing business, so always visit the publisher's Web site to learn the most up-to-date information, including the name of the editor to whom you should address your proposal. It is also a good idea to check the most up-to-date print guides mentioned earlier.

EXERCISES

1. Make a list of three or four individuals you've never heard of until you encountered their name in a work of history, or a in biography focus-

ing on someone else. Use the indexes and bibliographies to help you locate additional works (if any) about this person. Try locating information on the Web. Once you've gathered some information about these individuals, select one of them and prepare an outline for a book (see Exercise 2).

2. Prepare a working outline for a book-length lifewriting project, such as a biography of a little-known figure in history or an-depth look at people engaged in a seldom-discussed activity (bagel bakers? encryption specialists? animal psychologists? glass blowers?) Once you have your outline, write a detailed chapter-by-chapter synopsis of the book.

3. Work out an organizational scheme for your memoir, avoiding a linear chronology from birth until present day. Limit the scope to certain years, such as early childhood or adolescence, or geographically (where you lived during important stages in your life), or thematically (e.g., The Dreamer; the Realist; the Pioneer).

17

Anatomy of an Essay:
Joan Didion's "Marrying Absurd"

In 1967 Joan Didion, one of America's most accomplished essayists and novelists, published an essay about Las Vegas marriages. The essay appears in her collection, *Slouching toward Bethlehem* and has become something of a classic of social commentary.

Before you read the essay, I recommend you write an entry in your Daybook in response to one or more of the following prompts:

1. If you've ever visited Las Vegas, what is your lasting impression of it? Describe particulars—individual establishments (exterior or interior appearance, ambiance), employees, entertainers. Let your attitude toward Las Vegas be reflected in the way you describe these particulars.

2. If you've ever witnessed or participated in a Las Vegas wedding ceremony, describe your experience. Again, focus on particulars.

3. Reflect on wedding ceremonies in general, including your own as well as those you've attended or participated in. Which ceremony stands out (if one does) as most memorable, moving, unusual, somber, and/or beautiful? Why?

After you've written your daybook entry or entries, read "Marrying Absurd" straight through without glancing ahead to my commentary. It's important that you form your own impressions first. As soon as you finish reading the essay, write a response to it in your daybook. Basically, did you like it or dislike it, and why? If you had been invited by a magazine editor to write about marriage ceremonies in Las Vegas, how would *you* have approached the topic? Can you tell if anything has changed about Las Vegas weddings—in the nature of the ceremony, the legal requirements, etc., since Didion wrote her essay in 1967?

Now read the essay again, paragraph by paragraph, paying attention to the commentary that follows.

Marrying Absurd

To be married in Las Vegas, Clark County, Nevada, a bride must swear that she is eighteen or has parental permission and a bridegroom that he is twenty-one or has parental permission. Someone must put up five dollars for the license. (On Sundays and holidays, fifteen dollars. The Clark County Courthouse issues marriage licenses at any time of the day or night except between noon and one in the afternoon, between eight and nine in the evening, and between four and five in the morning.) Nothing else is required. The State of Nevada, alone among these United States, demands neither a premarital blood test nor a waiting period before or after the issuance of a marriage license. Driving in across the Mojave from Los Angeles, one sees the signs way out on the desert, looming up from the moonscape of rattlesnakes and mesquite, even before the Las Vegas lights appear like a mirage on the horizon: "GETTING MARRIED? Free License Information First Strip Exit." Perhaps the Las Vegas wedding industry achieved its peak operational efficiency between 9:00 P.M. and midnight of August 26, 1965, an otherwise unremarkable Thursday which happened to be, by Presidential order, the last day on which anyone could improve his draft status merely by getting married. One hundred and seventy-one couples were pronounced man and wife in the name of Clark Country and the State of Nevada that night, sixty-seven of them by a single justice of the peace, Mr. James A. Brennan. Mr. Brennan did one wedding at the Dunes and the other sixty-six in his office, and charged each couple eight dollars. One bride lent her veil to six others. "I got it down from five to three minutes," Mr. Brennan said later of his feat. "I could've married them en masse, but they're people, not cattle. People expect more when they get married."

What people who get married in Las Vegas actually do expect—what, in the largest sense, their "expectations" are—strikes one as a curious and self-contradictory business. Las Vegas is the most extreme and allegorical of American settlements, bizarre and beautiful in its venality and in its devotion to immediate gratification, a place the tone of which is set by mobsters and call girls and ladies' room attendants with amyl nitrate poppers in their uniform pockets. Almost everyone notes that there is no "time" in Las Vegas, no night and no day and no past and no future (no Las Vegas casino, however, has taken the obliteration of the ordinary time sense quite so far as Harold's Club in Reno, which for a while issued, at odd intervals in the day and night, mimeographed "bulletins" carrying news from the world outside); neither is there any logical sense of where one is. One is standing on a highway in the middle of a vast hostile desert looking at an eighty-foot sign which blinks "STARDUST" or "CAESAR'S PALACE." Yes, but what does that explain? This geographical implausibility reinforces the sense that what happens there has no connection with "real" life; Nevada cities like Reno and Carson are ranch towns, Western towns, places behind which there is some historical imperative. But Las Vegas seems to exist only in the eye of the beholder. All of which makes it an extraordinarily stimulating and interesting place, but an odd one in which to want to wear a candlelight satin Priscilla of Boston wedding dress with Chantilly lace insets, tapered sleeves and a detachable modified train.

And yet the Las Vegas wedding business seems to appeal to precisely that impulse. "Sincere and Dignified Since 1954," one wedding chapel advertises. There are nineteen such wedding chapels in Las Vegas, intensely competitive, each offering better, faster, and, by implication, more sincere services than the next: Our Photos Best Anywhere, Your Wedding on A Phonograph Record, Candlelight with Your Ceremony, Honeymoon Accommodations, Free Transportation from Your Motel to Courthouse to Chapel and Return to Motel, Religious or Civil Ceremonies, Dressing Rooms, Flowers, Rings, Announcements, Witnesses Available, and Ample Parking. All of these services, like most others in Las Vegas (sauna baths, payroll-check cashing, chinchilla coats for sale or rent) are offered twenty-four hours a day, seven days a week, presumably on the premise that marriage, like craps, is a game to be played when the table seems hot.

But what strikes one most about the Strip chapels, with their wishing wells and stained-glass paper windows and their artificial bouvardia, is that so much of their business is by no means a matter of simple convenience, of late-night liaisons between show girls and baby Crosbys. Of course there is some of that. (One night about eleven o'clock in Las Vegas I watched a bride in an orange mini dress and masses of flame-colored hair stumble from a Strip chapel on the arm of her bridegroom, who looked the part of the expendable nephew in movies like *Miami Syndicate*. "I gotta get the kids," the bride whimpered. "I gotta pick up the sitter, I gotta get to the midnight show." "What you gotta get," the bridegroom said, opening the door of a Cadillac Coupe de Ville and watching her crumple on the seat, "is sober.") But Las Vegas seems to offer something other than "convenience"; it is merchandising "niceness," the facsimile of proper ritual, to children who do not know how else to find it, how to make the arrangements, how to do it "right." All day and evening long on the Strip, one sees actual wedding parties, waiting under the harsh lights at a crosswalk, standing uneasily in the parking lot of the Frontier while the photographer hired by the Little Church of the West ("Wedding Place of the Stars") certifies the occasion, takes the picture: the bride in a veil and while satin pumps, the bridegroom usually in a white dinner jacket, and even an attendant or two, a sister or a best friend in hot-pink peau de soie, a flirtation veil, a carnation nosegay. "When I Fall in Love It Will Be Forever," the organist plays, and then a few bars of Lohengrin. The mother cries; the stepfather, awkward in his role, invites the chapel hostess to join them for a drink at the Sands. The hostess declines with a professional smile; she has already transferred her interest to the group waiting outside. One bride out, another in, and again the sign goes up on the chapel door: "One moment please—Wedding."

I sat next to one such wedding party in a Strip restaurant the last time I was in Las Vegas. The marriage had just taken place; the bride still wore her dress, the mother her corsage. A bored waiter poured out a few swallows of pink champagne ("on the house") for everyone but the bride, who was too young to be served. "You'll need something with more kick than that," the bride's father said with heavy jocularity to his new son-in-law; the ritual jokes about the wedding night had a certain Panglossian character, since the bride was clearly several months pregnant. Another round of pink champagne, this time not on the house, and the bride began to cry. "It was just as nice," she sobbed, "as I hoped and dreamed it would be."

Joan Didion, "Marrying Absurd." from *Slouching Toward Bethlehem*. New York: Farrar, Straus and Giroux, 1968.

Commentary

The purpose of this commentary is to give you a sense of how an attentive reading of an excellent piece of lifewriting can reveal much in the way of thematic and stylistic richness. Reading with this kind of attentiveness—because it helps to recognize and internalize artistic possibilities—will ultimately strengthen your own writing.

Title:

The title gives us a clue not only to the topic, but to Didion's approach to the topic. Readers' curiosity is immediately piqued; what can possibly be absurd about *marrying*? (assuming this is a serious essay, not a humorous one).

Paragraph 1:

The first two sentences seem straightforward reportage—but wait, the wording prompts the reader to wonder about two things: (1) Is age or parental permission the authorities' *only* concern? (2) Is *swearing* that one's age is true or that permission has been given the only form of validation? Although these questions are answered explicitly soon enough, the author, by being indirect at the outset, has injected just the right note of strangeness to enhance reader curiosity.

And then more strangeness: Halfway through the paragraph the emphasis shifts from explication to rather bizarre cinematic descriptions of the Mojave Desert between Los Angeles and Las Vegas—a billboard that asks, "Getting Married?" A billboard! The very icon of crude advertising used to hawk what many consider to be a sacred union—then adds to the crudity with an explanation that marriage license information may be obtained "at the first Strip exit." The reference of course is to the casino-hotel-lined stretch of South Las Vegas Boulevard known to as the Strip—but the word *strip* has other connotations that clash with traditional connotations of "marriage." Didion knows exactly what she is doing. These are the brush strokes of a master ironist. The rest of the paragraph compounds the irony by focusing on the crass commercialism of what marriage in Nevada has devolved into. Finally, she ends the paragraph with double-edged irony by quoting one of the justices of the peace, "I could have married them en masse, but they're people, not cattle," after bragging about how he shortened the time of each ceremony (there were, after all, sixty-six couples waiting!) "from five to three minutes."

Paragraph 2:

In this next paragraph, Didion shows her hand. She wishes to be explicit about her main idea (what we writing teachers like to refer to as her *thesis*): "Las Vegas is the most extreme and allegorical of American settlements, bizarre and beautiful in its venality and in its devotion to immediate gratification..." (ah, but if the sentence ended there, it would have been a letdown after the brilliance of the opening paragraph—but look what she does with the rest of that sentence: "...a place the tone of which is set by mobsters and call girls and ladies' room attendants with amyl nitrite poppers in their uniform pockets.") Abstraction gives way to imagery bordering on the grotesque. And for that reason it is, as she says, "an extraordinarily stimulating and interesting place"—especially from a writer's perspective—even though it makes us drop our assessment of the human condition a few notches.

Paragraph 3:

In this short paragraph Didion gets to the heart of what gives Vegas its peculiar nature: It is an unreal city that appeals to the human need for unreality.

Paragraph 4:

It is only with the penultimate paragraph that the narrator makes herself present. Why do you suppose she waited so long? Notice that the narrator is strictly an observer: "One night about eleven o'clock...I watched a bride in an orange mini dress and masses of flame-colored hair stumble from a Strip chapel on the arm of her bridegroom...." The fact that her observation of the drunken bride and bridegroom is in parentheses suggests that Didion wants to keep the incident in the larger context of Las

Vegas milieu—which is fine, but one possible criticism to Didion's approach is that by not moving in closer to the individuals involved—i.e., by not penetrating further into their lives—she runs the risk of oversimplifying. Why *do* people decide to marry in a place like Las Vegas? Perhaps there is a different—and complex—reason in each case.

In the rest of the paragraph, note how Didion plays with further irony, thereby reinforcing her theme of absurdity: In a ceremony that is squeezed in with dozens of others, that is hurried along, one member of a wedding party is singing "When I Fall in Love It Will Be Forever." Note the reference to the door sign in the especially effective last line that caps that irony: "One moment please—Wedding."

Paragraph 5:

This concluding paragraph is the shortest: one last incident in which the narrator, while still an outsider, sitting next to a new bride, and overhearing those typical cliches of all weddings—the bride's father's remark: "'You'll need something with more kick than that,'" followed by "'ritual jokes about the wedding night,'" and the bride's response used to end the essay: "'It was just as nice,' she sobbed, 'as I hoped and dreamed it would be.'"

In some ways this last paragraph is the most disturbing because Didion seems to be obliquely criticizing all weddings, not just Las Vegas ones—that what goes on in Vegas is simply a more condensed version of what goes on in statelier weddings, whether performed by a justice of the peace or by a priest or minister in a church. Is such a criticism warranted? Is there anything in the essay to justify such a stance? I leave that up to you to decide.

Recommended Reading
for Lifewriters

If you are a beginning writer, I cannot give you more important advice than to read extensively, as well as intensively. Not only read, but reread, so that the best writing gets under your skin. The following books represent a small sampling of the literary riches that await you, but they're a good starting point, and should keep you busy reading long enough for you to find a lot more on your own.

Essay Anthologies

- American Society of Magazine Editors, *The Best American Magazine Writing* [published annually since 2000]. Different guest editor each year. Twenty essays, more or less, selected from commercial magazines, such as *Harper's*, *Atlantic*, *Esquire*, *Vogue*, *Sports Illustrated*.

- Robert Atwan, series editor, *The Best American Essays* [published annually since 1986]. Different guest editor for each year. About twenty essays selected mainly from literary journals.

- Russell Baker, editor, *Russell Baker's Book of American Humor*. A rich selection of humorous and satirical writing from Mark Twain to the present day.

- Royce Flippin, editor, *The Best American Political Writing* 2002, [Inaugural annual collection] Lively political essays and articles from a variety of periodicals.

- Philip Lopate, editor, *The Art of the Personal Essay*. An excellent representation of the personal essay, from its ancient roots to the present day. Good representation of essays from different cultures.

- Joyce Carol Oates, editor. *The Best American Essays of the Century*. A distinguished novelist, essayist, and critic selects her choice for the best of the best. Presented chronologically, beginning with Mark Twain's "Corn-pone Opinions" in 1901. Fifty-five essays in all.

Essay Collections, Individual Essayists

- James Baldwin, *Collected Essays*. Powerful, lyrical essays by the distinguished novelist and playwright, about the experiences of a black man in America, and abroad, during the mid-twentieth century.

- Dave Barry, *Dave Barry is Not Making This Up*. My favorite among this Pulitzer-prize winning humorist's many books.

- Annie Dillard, *Teaching a Stone to Talk*. Encounters with uncanny natural phenomena by Pulitzer-prize winning author of *Pilgrim at Tinker Creek*, which one might describe as a natural-history memoir.

- Joseph Epstein, *With My Trousers Rolled: Familiar Essays*. Sixteen witty and somewhat eccentric personal essays, by a veteran literary critic, on topics like the delights of middle age, on being "out of it," and subjective time.

- Ron Hansen, *A Stay Against Confusion: Essays on Faith and Fiction*. Meditative essays that illuminate the subtle relationship between religious and literary experience, namely the act of story telling, from the Parables of Jesus to modern-day works of literature—by the author of *Mariette in Ecstasy*, *Atticus*, and *Isn't It Romantic?*

- Nancy Mairs, *Plaintext*. Essays on the experience of multiple sclerosis, womanhood, agoraphobia, sex. Also includes her most famous essay, "On Being a Cripple."

- Michel de Montaigne, *Selected Essays*. Collects the most memorable essays by the father of the essay, on such topics as friendship, books, smells, cannibals, the art of conversation, cruelty, and the education of children

- George Orwell, *A Collection of Essays*. Contains some of Orwell's most memorable pieces, such as "A Hanging," "Shooting an Elephant," "Politics and the English Language," and "Marrakech."

- Chet Raymo, *Natural Prayers*. Essays on the spiritual dimensions of the natural world by a noted astronomer and science columnist for *The Boston Globe*.

- Scott Russell Sanders, *Secrets of the Universe: Scenes from the Journey Home*. Memorable essays on topics ranging from being raised by an alcoholic father to encounters with animals in the wild.

Single-Subject Biographies

- David McCullough, *John Adams*. A richly detailed story of one of America's founding fathers and the second president. Winner of the Pulitzer prize.

- Carol Shields, *Jane Austen*. In this short but probing biography, Carol Shields, Pulitzer-prize winning author of *The Stone Diaries*, sheds light on the more private aspects of the cherished novelist's life.

- Brooke Kroeger, *Nellie Bly: Daredevil, Reporter, Feminist*. An in-depth portrait of a pioneer investigative journalist dubbed "the best reporter in America" at the time of her death in 1922 by the *New York Evening Journal*.

- *Remembering Cesar: The Legacy of Cesar Chavez*. Ann McGregor, compiler, Cindy Wathen, editor. Essays on the late founder of the United Farm Workers by Jerry Brown, Henry Cisneros,

Coretta Scott King, Edward James Olmos, Martin Sheen, and members of the Chavez family.

- Larry McMurtry, *Crazy Horse*. Story of the legendary Sioux warrior who led the Battle of Little Big Horn.

- Alfred Habegger, *My Wars Are Laid Away in Books: The Life of Emily Dickinson*. The most important biography—since Richard Sewall's *Life of Emily Dickinson* published in 1974—of America's greatest and most mysterious female poet.

- Albrecht Folsing, *Albert Einstein*. Considered to be the definitive biography of the greatest scientist of the twentieth century.

- Sherwin B. Nuland, *Leonardo da Vinci*. Nuland, a professor of surgery at Yale and a National Book Award winner (*How We Die*, 1994), examines some of the mysteries about Leonardo's life and art from the works themselves and from the artist-inventor's obsession with mathematics.

- Stefan Kanfer, *Groucho: The Life and Times of Julius Henry Marx*. A delightful biography. Kanfer includes many passages from Groucho's films and comedy routines.

- Sylvia Nasar, *A Beautiful Mind*. Winner of the National Book Critics Circle Award for Biography. Biography of John Nash, the controversial mathematician, economist, and winner of the Nobel Prize. Made into an award-winning film starring Russell Crowe.

- Tanya Agathocleous, *George Orwell: Battling Big Brother*. A short pictorial biography of the great journalist, essayist, and novelist famous for *Animal Farm* and 1984.

- Douglas Brinkley, *Rosa Parks*. Profile of a seamstress who, on December 1, 1955, refused to give up her seat to a white man on a bus in Montgomery Alabama, thereby setting the Civil Rights movement into high gear.

- Bobbie Ann Mason, *Elvis Presley*. A portrait of the King by a distinguished novelist (*In Country*), memoirist (*Clear Springs*), and fellow Southerner.

Multiple-Subject Biographies

- Kitty Ferguson, *Tycho & Kepler: The Unlikely Partnership that Forever Changed Our Understanding of the Heavens*. An intimate look at the two greatest—and eccentric—astronomers of the sixteenth century who paved the way to our modern understanding of the heavens.

- Susan Orlean, *The Bullfighter Checks Her Makeup: My Encounters with Extraordinary People*. Lively profiles of unusual people, originally published in *The New Yorker*, including Christina Sanchez, a bullfighter; Theresa McGregor, a Maui surfer; and Kabena Oppong, "the king and supreme ruler of the African Ashanti tribespeople," who lives in a two-bedroom apartment in New York and drives a cab.

- Claudia Roth Pierpont, *Passionate Minds: Women Rewriting the World*. Biographical profiles of twelve extraordinary women writers, grouped into three categories: those who have dealt with issues of sexual freedom, including Anais Nin, Olive Schreiner, and even Mae West; those who have focused on politics, including Ayn Rand, Doris Lessing, and Hannah Arendt; and those who have dealt with issues of race, including Zora Neale Hurston and Eudora Welty.

Autobiography, Memoirs & Other Modes of Lifewriting

- Maya Angelou, *I Know Why the Caged Bird Sings*. Lyrical and moving remembrances of growing up in rural Arkansas, by the distinguished African American poet and essayist.

- Rick Bragg, *All Over But the Shoutin'*. Bragg, who won the Pulitzer prize for journalism, writes about growing up in poverty in Alabama.

- Alan Clark, *Mrs. Thatcher's Minister: The Private Diaries of Alan Clark*. New York: Farrar, Straus and Giroux, 1993. Scandalous! What more can I say?

- H.D. [Hilda Doolittle], *Tribute to Freud*. One of the great imagist poets of the early twentieth century, describes her therapy sessions with the founder of psychoanalysis.

- Anne Fadiman, Ex Libris: *Confessions of a Common Reader*. An interconnected collection of autobiographical essays all focusing on the author's lifelong experiences with books and reading.

- M.F.K. Fisher, *The Art of Eating*. One of several books by the woman who raised food writing to the level of literature.

- Patricia Hampl, A *Romantic Education*. Houghton Mifflin Literary Fellowship Award Winner. A poet as well as memoirist, Hampl writes eloquently of her experiences in Czechoslovakia, her ancestral homeland.

- Carolyn G. Heilbrun, *The Last Gift of Time: Life beyond Sixty*. The author of the Amanda Cross mysteries and a major literary critic writes about the pleasures of her later years.

- Mary Karr, *The Liar's Club*. An emotional roller-coaster of a memoir about growing up in a Texas oil town. Winner of the PEN/Martha Albrand Award.

- Barry Lopez, *Arctic Dreams: Imagination and Desire in a Northern Landscape*. Winner of the American Book Award, these interconnected essays describe the author's experiences in the arctic island regions of Canada.

- Frances Mayes, *Under the Tuscan Sun*. The story of how two poets fell in love with Tuscany, where they purchased and renovated an abandoned house. Filled with recipes! Made into a movie starring Diane Lane.

- Frank McCourt, *Angela's Ashes*. Pulitzer prize for nonfiction, 1997. An artistically crafted memoir of growing up in impoverished, abusive, and sometimes comically absurd conditions in Limerick, Ireland.

- John McPhee, *Oranges*. You'll meet fascinating people in the orange industry, as well as learn more than you could ever imagine about oranges, orange growing, and harvesting in this book-length essay.

- N. Scott Momaday, *The Way to Rainy Mountain*. The Pulitzer-prize winning author, a Kiowa Indian, relates the migration stories and legends of his people.

- Malcolm X, *The Autobiography of Malcolm X*. A classic work by one of the key figures of the Civil Rights movement, written with the assistance of Alex Haley.

- John Muir, *The Story of My Boyhood and Youth*. One of the greatest American naturalists describes his growing-up years in Wisconsin.

- Azar Nafizi, *Reading Lolita in Tehran: A Memoir in Books*. An Iranian woman, now a professor at Johns Hopkins University in Baltimore, tells the story of how she and several other women in Iran would get together and read forbidden books. Her story is inseparable from the political and cultural upheavals of her native country during the 1980s and 90s.

- Nichelle Nichols, *Beyond Uhura: Star Trek and Other Memories*. The first African-American woman to play a starring role in prime time network television tells the story of her growing-up years and her experiences with "Star Trek" and its creator, Gene Roddenberry.

- Louise Rafkin, *Other People's Dirt: A Housecleaner's Curious Adventures*. What a housekeeper with a gift for writing is able to disclose about the private lives of ordinary (and not-so-ordinary) people, based on what they leave around the house for the housekeeper to clean up.

- Ruth Reichl, *Tender at the Bone: Growing Up at the Table*. A memoir (with recipes) from the perspective of preparing and serving meals. "If you watched people as they ate, you could find out who they were."

- Richard Rodriguez, *Hunger of Memory: The Education of Richard Rodriguez*. Rodriguez, who credits English-only classes in U.S. schools with his academic success, nonetheless suffers erosion of intimacy with his family and his Mexican heritage as a result

- Oliver Sacks, *Uncle Tungsten: Memories of a Chemical Boyhood*. The portrait of a distinguished neurologist as a young man growing up in London during WWII, in a family of doctors and scientists.

- Margaret A. Salinger, *Dream Catcher: A Memoir*. What it was like being raised by the most reclusive of great American writers, J.D. Salinger.

- William Saroyan, *Places Where I've Done Time*. A collection of amusing and irreverent autobiographical sketches connected to particular sites around the country—from the First Armenian Presbyterian Church in Fresno, California, to the Belasco Theater in New York City, to the Raphael Hotel in Paris.

- Fred Setterberg, *The Roads Taken: Travels through America's Literary Landscapes*. Winner of the Associated Writing Programs Award for Creative Nonfiction.

- Tobias Wolff, *This Boy's Life: A Memoir*. Named one of the 100 best nonfiction books of the twentieth century, Wolff powerfully recreates his wayward, coast-to-coast, high-mischief childhood in the 1950s.

Note: For a list of published diaries and notebooks, see Chapter 2.

Market Guides

- Kathryn Struckel Brogan, editor, *Writer's Market*. Annual compilation of submission guidelines for book and periodical publishers, literary agents, and writing competitions.

- Brigitte Phillips, Susan D. Klassen, and Doris Hall, editors, *The American Directory of Writer's Guidelines*, 3rd Edition. Collection of actual writer's guidelines prepared for freelancers by more than 1,400 book and periodical publishers in the United States.

- Barry Turner, *The Writer's Handbook*. Annual compilation of over 5,500 entries covering every area of creative writing.

- Len Fulton, *The International Directory of Little Magazines and Small Press*. More than 6,000 places to get your writings published.

Books about Writing

- Ray Bradbury, *Zen in the Art of Writing*. A delightful book on the passions of experiencing life as a writer. Includes "behind the scenes" tidbits about his work in Hollywood and his interactions with editors.

- Anne Lamott, *Bird by Bird: Some Instructions on Writing and Life*. Down-to-earth advice, engagingly presented, on how to manage your writing life. Chapter topics include "False Starts," "Shitty First Drafts," "Dialogue," "Perfectionism"—which Lamott calls "the voice of the oppressor"—and "Writer's Groups."

- Stephen Blake Mettee, editor, *The Portable Writer's Conference*. Dozens of informative articles on every facet of the writer's craft, including working with a literary agent, writing humor, fashioning characters from genealogy, running a home-based writing business, and understanding copyright laws.

- Stephen Blake Mettee, *The Fast Track Course on How to Write a Nonfiction Book Proposal*. Concise, to-the-point instruction on preparing a book proposal from a seasoned editor. Includes a sample proposal that worked, and sample agent and publisher contracts.

- Joyce Carol Oates, *The Faith of a Writer: Life, Craft, Art*. The prolific novelist, essayist, and critic discusses topics especially important to beginning writers, such as reading widely, the role of the unconscious in creativity, and tapping into the mysteries of human personality.

Index

About the Author

Fred D. White received his Ph.D. in English from the University of Iowa. Since 1980, White has been teaching writing at Santa Clara University where he is currently director of the Core Composition Program. In 1997, he received the Louis and Dorina Brutocao Award for Teaching Excellence. In addition to having published numerous essays, scholarly articles, and book reviews, he is the author of four textbooks on writing, most recently *The Well-Crafted Argument* (Houghton Mifflin Co.), coauthored with Simone Billings. Mr. White lives in San Mateo, California, with his wife, Therese (an attorney), and two loveable but unruly cats. Readers are cordially invited to write to him with questions or comments at **fwhite@scu.edu**.

More great Quill Driver Books' titles on writing & publishing!

The American Directory of
Writer's Guidelines, 4th Edition

**A Compilation of Information for Freelancers from
More than 1,500 Magazine Editors and Book Publishers**

—Compiled and Edited by Brigitte M. Phillips, Susan D. Klassen and Doris Hall

Perhaps the best-kept secret in the publishing industry is that many publishers—both periodical publishers and book publishers—make available writer's guidelines to assist would-be contributors. Written by the staff at each publishing house, these guidelines help writers target their submissions to the exact needs of the individual publisher. *The American Directory of Writer's Guidelines* is a compilation of the actual writer's guidelines for more than 1,500 publishers.

$29.95 ($45.00 *Canada*)
• ISBN 1-884956-40-8
(Replaces 3rd Edition, ISBN 1-884956-19-X)
• Indexed by topics

" *Unlike the entries in Writer's Market (Writer's Digest, annual), which edits the information supplied by publishers and prints it in a standard entry format, this new resource contains unedited self-descriptions of publications and publishing houses.* **"**
—Booklist

Damn!
Why Didn't I Write That?

A Book-of-the-Month Club, Quality Paperback Book Club, and Writer's Digest Book Club Selection!

**How Ordinary People are Raking in $100,000.00...
Or More Writing Nonfiction Books & How You Can Too!**

—by Marc McCutcheon

More nonfiction books are breaking the 100,000-copy sales barrier than ever before. Amateur writers, housewives, and even high school dropouts have cashed in with astonishingly simple best-sellers. This guide, by best-selling author Marc McCutcheon, shows the reader how to get in on the action.

$14.95 ($22.50 *Canada*)
• ISBN 1-884956-17-3

" *Comprehensive and engaging this book will save you time, energy, and frustration.* **"**
— Michael Larsen, literary agent, author

More great Quill Driver Books' titles on writing & publishing!

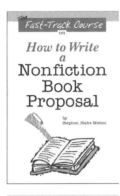

The Fast-Track Course
Nonfiction Book Proposal
—by Stephen Blake Mettee

Mettee, a seasoned book editor and publisher, cuts to the chase and provides simple, detailed instruction that allows anyone to write a professional book proposal and hear an editor say "Yes!"

$12.95 ($19.95 *Canada*)
• ISBN 1-884956-22-X

"*...essential, succinct guideline. This is a must have reference book for writers ...sets the industry standard.***"**
—Bob Spear, *Heartland Reviews*

"*Every writer needs a book like this. Mettee's sound, practical advice is just the ticket to make an editor welcome a writer's work! Keep the book close by, because you'll use it—guaranteed!***"**
—William Noble, author of *Writing Dramatic Nonfiction*

Both titles are Writer's Digest Book Club Selections!

Quit Your Day Job!
How to Sleep Late, Do What You Enjoy, and Make a Ton of Money *as a Writer!*
—by Jim Denney

Resolution and perseverance are required to build a writing career and if you're going to succeed, you don't need the hype or hyperbole so often dished out in other writer's guides. You need a candid, no-nonsense appraisal of the daily grind of the writer's life, with the potholes and pitfalls clearly marked.

This book is your road map, written by someone who's lived the writing life for years, with more than sixty published novels and nonfiction books to his credit.

$14.95 (29.95 *Canada*)
• ISBN 1-884956-04-1

"*While there are always a few charmed souls, most career-bent writers are destined to struggle. Jim Denney has been there, done that. Read his book and save yourself much of the anguish.***"**
—James N. Frey, author of *How to Write a Damn Good Novel*

Available at better brick and mortar bookstores, online bookstores, at QuillDriverBooks.com or by calling toll-free 1-800-497-4909

Still more great Quill Driver Books' titles on writing & publishing!

The ABCs of
Writing for Children
114 Children's Authors and Illustrators
**Talk About the Art, the Business, the Craft
& the Life of Writing Children's Literature**
—by Elizabeth Koehler-Pentacoff

A Writer's Digest Book Club Selection!

$14.95 *($22.95 Canada)*
• ISBN 1-884956-28-9

In *The ABCs of Writing for Children* you'll learn the many 'do's and don'ts' for creating children's books. You'll see that what works for one author may not work for the next.

❝ ...a thorough, complete, entertaining guide to writing for children—more alpha to omega than *ABCs*. I wish there was such a volume for every aspect of my life! ❞
—Karen Cushman, author of *Catherine, Called Birdy*

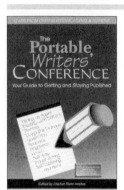

The Portable Writers' Conference
Your Guide to Getting and *Staying* Published
—Edited by Stephen Blake Mettee

Over 45 editors, authors, and agents advise writers on the art and business of writing and getting published. Chapters range from how to write a dynamite love scene to how to find an agent.

❝ Here is the perfect way to attend a writers' conference... ❞
—*Library Journal*

$19.95 *($29.95 Canada)* • ISBN 1-884956-23-8

Both titles are Writer's Digest Book Club Selections!

Feminine Wiles
**Creative Techniques for Writing
Women's Feature Stories That *Sell***
—by Donna Elizabeth Boetig

From *Feminine Wiles*: ...commit yourself. You are going to write stories of women's struggles and joys. You are going to discover information that changes the lives of readers. You are going to predict trends and you may even create a few of your own. You are going to look out into the world to see what's happening and take what you find deep within yourself to figure out what it all means—for you, and your readers.

❝ More valuable than a dozen writer's workshops or journalism courses. If you're interested in developing a successful career as a freelance writer for women's magazines, read *Feminine Wiles*—and get to work. ❞
— Jane Farrell, Senior Editor *McCall's*

$14.95 *($21.95 Canada)*
• ISBN 1-884956-02-5

Available at better brick and mortar bookstores, online bookstores, at
QuillDriverBooks.com or by calling toll-free 1-800-497-4909